Hesiod Theogony
800–700 BC

Birth of the Gods and Cosmos

Metaphrasis: Dimitrios Kiriakopoulos

Strategic Book Publishing and Rights Co.

Copyright © 2013

All rights reserved—Metaphrasis: Dimitrios Kiriakopoulos

No part of this book may be reproduced or transmitted in any form or by any means, graphic, electronic, or mechanical, including photocopying, recording, taping, or by any information storage retrieval system, without the permission, in writing, from the publisher.

Strategic Book Publishing and Rights Co.
12620 FM 1960, Suite A4-507
Houston, TX 77065
www.sbpra.com

ISBN: 978-1-62212-357-5

Design: Dedicated Book Services (www.netdbs.com)

Table of Contents

Synopsis-Intoduction iv
Quotations v
Note on the Spelling vi
Hesiod Biography vii
Major Works viii
Hesiod Theogony. 1
Notes 76
Related Extracts 85
On Isis and Osiris Plutarch 90
About the Author 93

Synopsis-Intoduction

Theogony is a charming and amusing story, the longest of the three surviving works of Hesiod. It consists of 1022 verses and describes the creation of the cosmos and the birth of the gods. It may be divided in five parts. The first section is the introduction from 1–115, where Hesiod is authorized by the Mousai to hear the story of the universal creation and is inspired by them, whereupon he composed the poem. Admitting that he heard the story from them and that it is not his own invention, we might say that he is more like the publisher than the author.

From 116–210 is the creation of the universe from Khaos along with all the elements and the first deities; this is Ouranos's (sky) era. From 211–496 is where Kronos overthrows Ouranos and reigns for a long period of time without justice and evil prevails.

497–965 is Zeus's era, when with his strength he took over the power from Kronos and overcoming the Titans, and bound them in Tartaros. The conclusion is from 966 to the end, as immortal goddesses join with mortal men, creating the race of the demigods and heroes, an era which ends right after the Trojan War.

Zeus has the main role in the story, being the creator and the leader of the universal civilization. His weddings with Metis, Themis, Mnemosyne, and Eurynome, who represent law, institutions, and justice, allowed him to create the basis for serenity and prosperity of the cosmos. As for today, when the world is scourged with the paranoia of the magistrates, Zeus, the greatest bright mind, continues to be the supreme model of a leader.

Quotations

"The study of mythology need no longer be looked at as an escape from reality into the fantasies of primitive peoples, but as a search for the deeper understanding of the human mind. In reaching out to explore the distant hills where the gods dwell and the deeps where the monsters are lurking, we are perhaps discovering the way home."

–H. R. Ellis Davidson

"That the myths are divine can be seen from those who have used them. Myths have been used by inspired poets, by the best of philosophers, by those who established the mysteries, and by the Gods themselves in oracles. But why the myths are divine it is the duty of philosophy to inquire. Since all existing things rejoice in that which is like them and reject that which is unlike, the stories about the Gods ought to be like the Gods, so that they may both be worthy of the divine essence and make the Gods well disposed to those who speak of them: which could only be done by means of myths."

—Salustius

Note on the Spelling

By transliterating the names, we are maintaining their character, authenticity, and identity. I have withdrawn all the Cs (a Latin convention) from their spelling, since that letter didn't exist in Greek (e.g., Khaos instead of Chaos), and also replaced the ending "-us" of the masculine names with "-os" (e.g., Krios for Crius), since there is not such an ending in Greek. An exception is the ending diphthong "-eus" (Z-eus, Pers-eus) which is pronounced as "-efs."

Hesiod Biography

The Greek poet Hesiod (800–700 BC) was the first didactic poet in Europe and the first author of mainland Greece whose works are extant. His influence on later literature was basic and far-reaching.

Biographical facts about Hesiod are shrouded in myth and the obscurity of time; what we can say with certainty about him comes from his own writing. His father, a merchant, migrated from Cyme in Asia Minor and became a farmer near the town of Ascra in Boeotia, where Hesiod lived most or all of his life. Hesiod undoubtedly spent his early years working his father's land. After his father's death Hesiod was involved in a bitter dispute with his brother, Perses, over the division of the property. Later legend relates that Hesiod moved from Ascra and that he was murdered in Oenoe in Locris for having seduced a maiden; their child is said to have been the lyric poet Stesichorus. Hesiod relates that the only time he traveled across the sea was to compete in a poetry contest at the funeral games of Amphidamas at Chalcis (in Euboea).

The dates of Hesiod's life are much disputed. Some of the ancient chroniclers make him a contemporary of Homer; most modern critics date his activity not long after the Homeric epics but presumably before 700 BC. The titles of a number of poems have come down to us under the name of Hesiod, but only two complete works survive which are generally believed to be genuine.

Major Works

The *Theogony* (*Theogonia*, or Genealogy of the Gods) is a 1022-line narrative description of the origin of the universe and the gods.

Although many of the myths which Hesiod incorporates are extremely primitive and probably Eastern in origin, the Theogony is a successful attempt to give a rational and coherent explanation of the formation and government of the universe from its primal origins through the ultimate mastery of the cosmos by Zeus, "the father of men and gods." Of special interest in the *Theogony* are the vivid descriptions of battles between the gods and the Titans.

The *Works and Days* (*Erga Kai Hemerai*), another long poem (over 800 lines), is much more personal in tone. It is addressed to Hesiod's brother, Perses, who had taken the bigger portion of their inheritance by means of bribes to the local "kings" and later squandered it. Around this theme of admonition to his brother Hesiod composed a didactic poem consisting of practical advice to farmers and seafarers, maxims (again, mostly practical) on how to conduct oneself in everyday affairs with fellow men, moral and ethical precepts, and warnings to the local "kings" to observe righteousness in their disposition of justice. A long section at the end is a list of primitive taboos followed by a catalog of lucky and unlucky days. The authenticity of these lines is doubted, but they are characteristic of the unsophisticated peasant outlook.

The two major themes that Hesiod sounds again and again are the necessity for all men to be just and fair, since justice comes from Zeus, who will punish the wrongdoer, and the formula that success depends on unceasing hard work. If you desire wealth, Hesiod says, then "work with work upon work." The world which Hesiod describes in the *Works and Days* is not the heroic arena of the Trojan War but the difficult life of the small peasant farmer. Hesiod's view is essentially pessimistic. Ascra, his home, is "bad in winter, harsh in summer, good at no time." In one famous passage, he details the five "Ages of Man." From the Golden Age of the reign of Kronos through the Silver, Bronze, and Brass ages of heroes, mankind has degenerated. Hesiod finds himself in the Age of Iron, where there is nothing but trouble and sorrow, labor and strife. Also included in the *Works and Days* is the story of Pandora, the first woman. The myth states that she was created at Zeus's command as a punishment for men.

Other Works

A number of other poems, attributed to Hesiod in antiquity and now generally ascribed to the "Boeotian," or "Hesiodic," school, are known by title or from fragmentary remains. The most important of these "minor works," possibly by Hesiod himself, was the *Catalog of Women*, which seems to have described the loves of the gods and their offspring. A number of fragmentary excerpts survive. A longer fragment, called the *Shield of Herakles*, most likely not by Hesiod, narrates the battle between Herakles and the robber Kyknos. A large portion of this substantial (480 lines) fragment is devoted to a description of Herakles's shield—an inferior imitation of the famous description in the *Iliad* of the shield of Achilles.

Like Homer, Hesiod wrote in the Ionian dialect and employed the dactylic hexameter, the meter of the epic poets, but the soaring elegance of the Homeric poems is replaced by a simpler, more earthy style. Portions of the Hesiodic poems are mere catalogs of names and events, but often his words ring with an eloquence and conviction that reveal true literary genius. Hesiod was the first European poet to speak in a personal vein and to stress social and moral ethics. The *Theogony* won immediate acceptance as the authentic account of Greek cosmogony, and it stands today as one of the important basic documents for the study of Greek mythology. Hesiod's professed intent was to instruct and inform, not to amuse; thus he stands at the head of a long line of teacher-poets in the Western world.

Ἡσίοδος
Θεογονία

Μουσάων Ἑλικωνιάδων ἀρχώμεθ᾽ ἀείδειν,
αἵ θ᾽ Ἑλικῶνος ἔχουσιν ὄρος μέγα τε ζάθεόν τε
καί τε περὶ κρήνην ἰοειδέα πόσσ᾽ ἁπαλοῖσιν
ὀρχεῦνται καὶ βωμὸν ἐρισθενέος Κρονίωνος·
καί τε λοεσσάμεναι τέρενα χρόα Περμησσοῖο　　　　　5
ἢ Ἵππου κρήνης ἢ Ὀλμειοῦ ζαθέοιο
ἀκροτάτῳ Ἑλικῶνι χοροὺς ἐνεποιήσαντο
καλούς, ἱμερόεντας· ἐπερρώσαντο δὲ ποσσίν.
Ἔνθεν ἀπορνύμεναι, κεκαλυμμέναι ἠέρι πολλῇ,
ἐννύχιαι στεῖχον περικαλλέα ὄσσαν ἱεῖσαι,　　　　　10
ὑμνεῦσαι Δία τ᾽ αἰγίοχον καὶ πότνιαν Ἥρην
Ἀργείην, χρυσέοισι πεδίλοις ἐμβεβαυῖαν,
κούρην τ᾽ αἰγιόχοιο Διὸς γλαυκῶπιν Ἀθήνην
Φοῖβόν τ᾽ Ἀπόλλωνα καὶ Ἄρτεμιν ἰοχέαιραν
ἠδὲ Ποσειδάωνα γαιήοχον, ἐννοσίγαιον,　　　　　15
καὶ Θέμιν αἰδοίην ἑλικοβλέφαρόν τ᾽ Ἀφροδίτην
Ἥβην τε χρυσοστέφανον καλήν τε Διώνην
Λητώ τ᾽ Ἰαπετόν τε ἰδὲ Κρόνον ἀγκυλομήτην
Ἠῶ τ᾽ Ἠέλιόν τε μέγαν λαμπράν τε Σελήνην
Γαῖάν τ᾽ Ὠκεανόν τε μέγαν καὶ Νύκτα μέλαιναν　　　　　20
ἄλλων τ᾽ ἀθανάτων ἱερὸν γένος αἰὲν ἐόντων.
Αἵ νύ ποθ᾽ Ἡσίοδον καλὴν ἐδίδαξαν ἀοιδήν,

Hesiod
Theogony

Of the Helikoniadai Mousai, we begin to sing,

the Mousai who hold the great and sacred mount of Helikon*

and dance on gentle feet• 'round the violet-blue spring

and also the altar of the almighty son of Kronos

and when they have washed their soft bodies in the spring of Permessos　　　　5

or in the Horse's spring or the divine Olmeios,

upon the top of Helikon beautiful and charming dances they start

with all their strength on their feet.

From here they start up, covered in thick mist

and nightly they march and utter their hymn,　　　　10

with lovely voices praising the aegiokhos Zeus and queenly Hera of Argos

who walks on golden sandals,

and the daughter of the aegiokhos Zeus, glaukopis Athena*

and Phoebos Apollo and Artemis the arrow shooter

and Poseidon the earth-holder and earth-shaker　　　　15

and the respectful Themis and the quick-glancing Aphrodite

and Hebe with the golden crown and pretty Dione,

Leto and Iapetos and Kronos the crooked,

Eos and great Helios and bright Selene,

Gaia (Earth) and the great Okeanos (Ocean), the black Night　　　　20

and the divine race of all the immortals who are forever.

They, one day, taught Hesiod a great song*

2 Metaphrasis: Dimitrios Kiriakopoulos

ἄρνας ποιμαίνονθ' Ἑλικῶνος ὕπο ζαθέοιο.

Τόνδε δέ με πρώτιστα θεαὶ πρὸς μῦθον ἔειπον,

Μοῦσαι Ὀλυμπιάδες, κοῦραι Διὸς αἰγιόχοιο·   25

«Ποιμένες ἄγραυλοι, κάκ' ἐλέγχεα, γαστέρες οἶον,

ἴδμεν ψεύδεα πολλὰ λέγειν ἐτύμοισιν ὁμοῖα,

ἴδμεν δ', εὖτ' ἐθέλωμεν, ἀληθέα γηρύσασθαι.»

Ὣς ἔφασαν κοῦραι μεγάλου Διὸς ἀρτιέπειαι·

καί μοι σκῆπτρον ἔδον δάφνης ἐριθηλέος ὄζον   30

δρέψασαι, θηητόν· ἐνέπνευσαν δέ μοι ἀοιδὴν

θέσπιν, ἵνα κλείοιμι τά τ' ἐσσόμενα πρό τ' ἐόντα.

Καί μ' ἐκέλονθ' ὑμνεῖν μακάρων γένος αἰὲν ἐόντων,

σφᾶς δ' αὐτὰς πρῶτόν τε καὶ ὕστατον αἰὲν ἀείδειν.

Ἀλλὰ τί ἦ μοι ταῦτα περὶ δρῦν ἢ περὶ πέτρην;   35

Τύνη, Μουσάων ἀρχώμεθα, ταὶ Διὶ πατρὶ

ὑμνεῦσαι τέρπουσι μέγαν νόον ἐντὸς Ὀλύμπου,

εἰρεῦσαι τά τ' ἐόντα τά τ' ἐσσόμενα πρό τ' ἐόντα,

φωνῇ ὁμηρεῦσαι· τῶν δ' ἀκάματος ῥέει αὐδὴ

ἐκ στομάτων ἡδεῖα· γελᾷ δέ τε δώματα πατρὸς   40

Ζηνὸς ἐριγδούποιο θεᾶν ὀπὶ λειριοέσσῃ

σκιδναμένῃ· ἠχεῖ δὲ κάρη νιφόεντος Ὀλύμπου

δώματά τ' ἀθανάτων. Αἳ δ' ἄμβροτον ὄσσαν ἱεῖσαι

θεῶν γένος αἰδοῖον πρῶτον κλείουσιν ἀοιδῇ

ἐξ ἀρχῆς, οὓς Γαῖα καὶ Οὐρανὸς εὐρὺς ἔτικτεν,   45

οἵ τ' ἐκ τῶν ἐγένοντο θεοί, δωτῆρες ἑάων.

Δεύτερον αὖτε Ζῆνα, θεῶν πατέρ' ἠδὲ καὶ ἀνδρῶν,

ἀρχόμεναί θ' ὑμνεῦσι θεαὶ λήγουσαί τ' ἀοιδῆς,

ὅσσον φέρτατός ἐστι θεῶν κράτεΐ τε μέγιστος.

while he was shepherding lambs under the holy Helikon.

This story the goddesses first said to me,

the Olympian Mousai, the daughters of aegiokhos Zeus: 25

"Shepherds, dwellers of the fields, base reproaches, bellies only,

we know to say many lies which appear to be true,

but when we want, we also know how to speak the truth." *

This is how they spoke to me, the glib daughters of great Zeus,

and they gave me a sceptre, cutting a branch of a well-flourishing laurel, 30

admirable. They breathed into me a divine voice*

to celebrate things that will come and things that have passed

and told me to sing of the eternal race of the blessed gods

but also to sing of themselves first and last.

But why all of this around an oak and a stone?* 35

Come then, let us begin with the Mousai who with their songs

gladden the great spirit of their father Zeus within Olympos,

telling of things that are and will be and were before,*

in harmonic voice. From their lips flows song sweet and untiring

and glad is the house of their father, Zeus the loud-thunderer. 40

As it spreads abroad with the delicate voice of the goddesses,

the summit of snowy Olympos and the homes of the immortals echo.

And they, lifting their immortal voices in song, they celebrate first of all

the reverent race of the gods, beginning with those

whom Gaia and the wide Ouranos brought into the world 45

and the gods who sprung of them, givers of goods.

Then, next, they sing of Zeus, the father of gods and men,

as they begin and end their ode,

how the bravest and most powerful he is amongst the gods.

4   Metaphrasis: Dimitrios Kiriakopoulos

Αὖτις δ᾽ ἀνθρώπων τε γένος κρατερῶν τε Γιγάντων   50

ὑμνεῦσαι τέρπουσι Διὸς νόον ἐντὸς Ὀλύμπου

Μοῦσαι Ὀλυμπιάδες, κοῦραι Διὸς αἰγιόχοιο.

Τὰς ἐν Πιερίῃ Κρονίδῃ τέκε πατρὶ μιγεῖσα

Μνημοσύνη, γουνοῖσιν Ἐλευθῆρος μεδέουσα,

λησμοσύνην τε κακῶν ἄμπαυμά τε μερμηράων.   55

Ἐννέα γάρ οἱ νυκτὸς ἐμίσγετο μητίετα Ζεὺς

νόσφιν ἀπ᾽ ἀθανάτων ἱερὸν λέχος εἰσαναβαίνων·

ἀλλ᾽ ὅτε δή ῥ᾽ ἐνιαυτὸς ἔην, περὶ δ᾽ ἔτραπον ὧραι

μηνῶν φθινόντων, περὶ δ᾽ ἤματα πόλλ᾽ ἐτελέσθη,

ἣ δ᾽ ἔτεκ᾽ ἐννέα κούρας ὁμόφρονας, ᾗσιν ἀοιδὴ   60

μέμβλεται ἐν στήθεσσιν, ἀκηδέα θυμὸν ἐχούσαις,

τυτθὸν ἀπ᾽ ἀκροτάτης κορυφῆς νιφόεντος Ὀλύμπου.

[Ἔνθα σφιν λιπαροί τε χοροὶ καὶ δώματα καλά.

Πὰρ δ᾽ αὐτῇς Χάριτές τε καὶ Ἵμερος οἰκί᾽ ἔχουσιν

ἐν θαλίῃς· ἐρατὴν δὲ διὰ στόμα ὄσσαν ἱεῖσαι   65

μέλπονται πάντων τε νόμους καὶ ἤθεα κεδνὰ

ἀθανάτων κλείουσιν, ἐπήρατον ὄσσαν ἱεῖσαι.]

Αἳ τότ᾽ ἴσαν πρὸς Ὄλυμπον ἀγαλλόμεναι ὀπὶ καλῇ,

ἀμβροσίῃ μολπῇ· περὶ δ᾽ ἴαχε γαῖα μέλαινα

ὑμνεύσαις, ἐρατὸς δὲ ποδῶν ὕπο δοῦπος ὀρώρει   70

νισσομένων πατέρ᾽ ὅν· ὃ δ᾽ οὐρανῷ ἐμβασιλεύει,

αὐτὸς ἔχων βροντὴν ἠδ᾽ αἰθαλόεντα κεραυνόν,

κάρτεϊ νικήσας πατέρα Κρόνον· εὖ δὲ ἕκαστα

ἀθανάτοις διέταξεν ὁμῶς καὶ ἐπέφραδε τιμάς.

Ταῦτ᾽ ἄρα Μοῦσαι ἄειδον, Ὀλύμπια δώματ᾽ ἔχουσαι,   75

ἐννέα θυγατέρες μεγάλου Διὸς ἐκγεγαυῖαι,

And again, they sing for the race of men and the powerful giants

and satisfy the heart of Zeus in Olympos,

the Olympian Mousai, daughters of aegiokhos Zeus.

Them in Pieria, Mnemosyne (memory), the guardian of the hills of Eleutherai,

brought into the world in union with the son of Kronos

to be a forgetting of bad and a resting of trouble.

For nine nights, all-wise Zeus was mingled with the goddess Mnemosyne,

getting on her holy bed far from the immortals.

And when the cycle of time did close and the hours came around,

as the months came to an end and the days passed by,

she bore nine daughters, all of one mind, on whose hearts song is a care

and their spirit is free of sorrow,

a little way from the highest peak of snowy Olympos,

where there are for them brilliant dancing places and beautiful homes.

Beside them, the Graces and Himeros live in a house with abundance.

Issuing charming sounds from their lips,

celebrating with song and dance, singing the laws of all

and the sage ethos of the immortals, uttering in lovely voice.

They went to Olympos with delight for their sweet tone and the divine song,

and around them, as they chanted, the dark Gaia echoed

And beneath their feet, heavy sound rose up

as they went to their father, who is the king of the sky,

and only himself is holding the thunderbolt and the burning lightning,

after he had by power overcome his father Kronos.

In good order he did put the things of the immortals and distributed their rewards.

These things, the Mousai who dwell in the Olympian halls were singing,

the nine daughters born by great Zeus.*

6 Metaphrasis: Dimitrios Kiriakopoulos

Κλειώ τ' Εὐτέρπη τε Θάλειά τε Μελπομέενη τε

Τερψιχόρη τ' Ἐρατώ τε Πολύμνιά τ' Οὐρανίη τε

Καλλιόπη θ'· ἣ δὲ προφερεστάτη ἐστὶν ἁπασέων.

Ἥ γὰρ καὶ βασιλεῦσιν ἅμ' αἰδοίοισιν ὀπηδεῖ.   80

Ὅν τινα τιμήσωσι Διὸς κοῦραι μεγάλοιο,

γεινόμενόν τε ἴδωσι διοτρεφέων βασιλήων,

τῷ μὲν ἐπὶ γλώσσῃ γλυκερὴν χείουσιν ἐέρσην,

τοῦ δ' ἔπε' ἐκ στόματος ῥεῖ μείλιχα· οἱ δέ τε λαοὶ

πάντες ἐς αὐτὸν ὁρῶσι διακρίνοντα θέμιστας   85

ἰθείῃσι δίκῃσιν· ὃ δ' ἀσφαλέως ἀγορεύων

αἶψά κε καὶ μέγα νεῖκος ἐπισταμένως κατέπαυσεν·

τοὔνεκα γὰρ βασιλῆες ἐχέφρονες, οὕνεκα λαοῖς

βλαπτομένοις ἀγορῆφι μετάτροπα ἔργα τελεῦσι

ῥηιδίως, μαλακοῖσι παραιφάμενοι ἐπέεσσιν.   90

Ἐρχόμενον δ' ἀν' ἀγῶνα θεὸν ὣς ἱλάσκονται

αἰδοῖ μειλιχίῃ, μετὰ δὲ πρέπει ἀγρομένοισιν·

τοίη Μουσάων ἱερὴ δόσις ἀνθρώποισιν.

Ἐκ γάρ τοι Μουσέων καὶ ἑκηβόλου Ἀπόλλωνος

ἄνδρες ἀοιδοὶ ἔασιν ἐπὶ χθόνα καὶ κιθαρισταί,   95

ἐκ δὲ Διὸς βασιλῆες· ὃ δ' ὄλβιος, ὅν τινα Μοῦσαι

φίλωνται· γλυκερή οἱ ἀπὸ στόματος ῥέει αὐδή.

Εἰ γάρ τις καὶ πένθος ἔχων νεοκηδέι θυμῷ

ἄζηται κραδίην ἀκαχήμενος, αὐτὰρ ἀοιδὸς

Μουσάων θεράπων κλέεα προτέρων ἀνθρώπων   100

ὑμνήσῃ μάκαράς τε θεούς, οἳ Ὄλυμπον ἔχουσιν,

αἶψ' ὅ γε δυσφροσυνέων ἐπιλήθεται οὐδέ τι κηδέων

μέμνηται· ταχέως δὲ παρέτραπε δῶρα θεάων.

Kleio, Euterpe, Thaleia, and Melpomene*
Terpsikhore, Erato, Polymnia, Ourania
and Kalliope, the superior of all,
for she attends the worshipful kings. 80
Whomever, of the cherished by Zeus kings, the daughters of great Zeus honor
and see at the time he is born,
they pour sweet dew upon his tongue
and from his lips row soothing words and all the people regard him,
as he, with just resolutions, hears their disputes. 85
As he speaks without faltering,
the great quarrels are quickly put to an end.
Then the kings are prudent when at the people's assembly,
easily they offer relief with encouraging and gentle words
and they turn 'round the deeds on behalf of the damaged. 90
Coming to the assembly, they greet him as god with gentle reverence
and he is distinguished in the gathering.
Such is the holy gift of the Mousai to people
because from them and the skilled archer Apollo
come to earth the singers and the guitarists, 95
since the kings come from Zeus. Happy is he whom the Mousai love
and sweet speech flows from his lips.
If someone has sorrow in his soul, whose grief is fresh
and whose heart dries up from mourning, when the singer—the attendant of Mousai—
sings the glory of the men of former times 100
and of the blessed gods who possess Olympos,
the mourner at once forgets his anxiety and doesn't remember his troubles at all,
so rapidly do the gifts of Mousai change his mind.

8   Metaphrasis: Dimitrios Kiriakopoulos

Χαίρετε, τέκνα Διός, δότε δ' ἱμερόεσσαν ἀοιδήν.

Κλείετε δ' ἀθανάτων ἱερὸν γένος αἰὲν ἐόντων,   105

οἳ Γῆς τ' ἐξεγένοντο καὶ Οὐρανοῦ ἀστερόεντος,

Νυκτός τε δνοφερῆς, οὕς θ' ἁλμυρὸς ἔτρεφε Πόντος.

Εἴπατε δ', ὡς τὰ πρῶτα θεοὶ καὶ γαῖα γένοντο

καὶ ποταμοὶ καὶ πόντος ἀπείριτος, οἴδματι θυίων,

ἄστρα τε λαμπετόωντα καὶ οὐρανὸς εὐρὺς ὕπερθεν   110

οἵ τ' ἐκ τῶν ἐγένοντο θεοί, δωτῆρες ἐάων

ὥς τ' ἄφενος δάσσαντο καὶ ὡς τιμὰς διέλοντο

ἠδὲ καὶ ὡς τὰ πρῶτα πολύπτυχον ἔσχον Ὄλυμπον.

Ταῦτά μοι ἔσπετε Μοῦσαι, Ὀλύμπια δώματ' ἔχουσαι

[ἐξ ἀρχῆς, καὶ εἴπαθ', ὅ τι πρῶτον γένετ' αὐτῶν.]   115

Ἤ τοι μὲν πρώτιστα Χάος γένετ', αὐτὰρ ἔπειτα

Γαῖ' εὐρύστερνος, πάντων ἕδος ἀσφαλὲς αἰεὶ

[ἀθανάτων, οἳ ἔχουσι κάρη νιφόεντος Ὀλύμπου,

Τάρταρά τ' ἠερόεντα μυχῷ χθονὸς εὐρυοδείης,]

ἠδ' Ἔρος, ὃς κάλλιστος ἐν ἀθανάτοισι θεοῖσι,   120

λυσιμελής, πάντων δὲ θεῶν πάντων τ' ἀνθρώπων

δάμναται ἐν στήθεσσι νόον καὶ ἐπίφρονα βουλήν.

Ἐκ Χάεος δ' Ἔρεβός τε μέλαινά τε Νὺξ ἐγένοντο·

Νυκτὸς δ' αὖτ' Αἰθήρ τε καὶ Ἡμέρη ἐξεγένοντο,

οὓς τέκε κυσαμένη Ἐρέβει φιλότητι μιγεῖσα.   125

Γαῖα δέ τοι πρῶτον μὲν ἐγείνατο ἶσον ἑ' αὐτῇ

Οὐρανὸν ἀστερόενθ', ἵνα μιν περὶ πάντα καλύπτοι,

ὄφρ' εἴη μακάρεσσι θεοῖς ἕδος ἀσφαλὲς αἰεί.

Γείνατο δ' Οὔρεα μακρά, θεῶν χαρίεντας ἐναύλους,

[Νυμφέων, αἳ ναίουσιν ἀν' οὔρεα βησσήεντα.]   130

Welcome children of Zeus! Give charming ode!
Celebrate the holy race of the immortals who are forever, 105
these who were born from Gaia and starry Ouranos
and the gloomy Night and the ones who the salty sea did feed.
Tell how first gods and the earth came into being
and the rivers and the boundless Sea, who is raging with swollen waves
and the shining stars and the wide sky above 110
and the gods who were born of them, givers of good things,
and how they divided the wealth among them and how they shared their honors,
also, how at first they possessed illustrious Olympos with the many folds.
These things, tell me from the beginning, oh Mousai,
dwellers of the Olympian halls, and tell me which one of them first came to be.* 115
First of all, Khaos came into being,*
but afterwards, Gaia the broad-breasted, a firm dwelling place for ever
of all the immortals who hold the summit of the snowy Olympos
and murky Tartaros, the inmost of the broad-pathed Gaia
and Eros,• the fairest of the immortal gods, 120
the limb-relaxing, who tames the mind in the chest
and also, the wise counsels of all gods and men.
From Khaos came into being Erebos and black Night
and from the Night came Aether (upper air) and Day,
whom she conceived and bore from union with Erebos, when she fell in love with him. 125
Gaia then first bore starry Ouranos, equal to herself,
to cover her on every side, in order to be
an ever-safe sanctuary for the blessed gods.
She brought forth the long mountains, graceful haunts
of the goddess-Nymphs, who dwell in the mountain glens. 130

10   Metaphrasis: Dimitrios Kiriakopoulos

Ἡ δὲ καὶ ἀτρύγετον πέλαγος τέκεν, οἴδματι θυῖον,

Πόντον, ἄτερ φιλότητος ἐφιμέρου· αὐτὰρ ἔπειτα

Οὐρανῷ εὐνηθεῖσα τέκ᾽ Ὠκεανὸν βαθυδίνην,

Κοῖόν τε Κρῖόν θ᾽ Ὑπερίονά τ᾽ Ἰαπετόν τε

Θείαν τε ῾Ρείαν τε Θέμιν τε Μνημοσύνην τε   135

Φοίβην τε χρυσοστέφανον Τηθύν τ᾽ ἐρατεινήν.

Τοὺς δὲ μέθ᾽ ὁπλότατος γένετο Κρόνος ἀγκυλομήτης,

δεινότατος παίδων· θαλερὸν δ᾽ ἤχθηρε τοκῆα.

Γείνατο δ᾽ αὖ Κύκλωπας ὑπέρβιον ἦτορ ἔχοντας,

Βρόντην τε Στερόπην τε καὶ Ἄργην ὀβριμόθυμον,   140

[οἳ Ζηνὶ βροντήν τε δόσαν τεῦξάν τε κεραυνόν.]

Οἳ δή τοι τὰ μὲν ἄλλα θεοῖς ἐναλίγκιοι ἦσαν,

μοῦνος δ᾽ ὀφθαλμὸς μέσσῳ ἐνέκειτο μετώπῳ.

[Κύκλωπες δ᾽ ὄνομ᾽ ἦσαν ἐπώνυμον, οὕνεκ᾽ ἄρα σφέων

κυκλοτερὴς ὀφθαλμὸς ἔεις ἐνέκειτο μετώπῳ·]   145

ἰσχὺς δ᾽ ἠδὲ βίη καὶ μηχαναὶ ἦσαν ἐπ᾽ ἔργοις.

Ἄλλοι δ᾽ αὖ Γαίης τε καὶ Οὐρανοῦ ἐξεγένοντο

τρεῖς παῖδες μεγάλοι τε καὶ ὄβριμοι, οὐκ ὀνομαστοί,

Κόττος τε Βριάρεώς τε Γύης θ᾽, ὑπερήφανα τέκνα.

Τῶν ἑκατὸν μὲν χεῖρες ἀπ᾽ ὤμων ἀίσσοντο,   150

ἄπλαστοι, κεφαλαὶ δὲ ἑκάστῳ πεντήκοντα

ἐξ ὤμων ἐπέφυκον ἐπὶ στιβαροῖσι μέλεσσιν·

ἰσχὺς δ᾽ ἄπλητος κρατερὴ μεγάλῳ ἐπὶ εἴδει.

Ὅσσοι γὰρ Γαίης τε καὶ Οὐρανοῦ ἐξεγένοντο,

δεινότατοι παίδων, σφετέρῳ δ᾽ ἤχθοντο τοκῆι   155

ἐξ ἀρχῆς· καὶ τῶν μὲν ὅπως τις πρῶτα γένοιτο,

πάντας ἀποκρύπτασκε, καὶ ἐς φάος οὐκ ἀνίεσκε,

She bore with Pontos, without desire or love,

the unfruitful open Sea, raging with swollen waves.

But afterwards, she laid with Ouranos and she bore deep-eddying Okeanos,

Koios and Krios and Hyperion and Iapetos,

Theia and Rhea and Themis and Mnemosyne, 135

the gold-crowned Phoebe and lovely Tethys.

After them was born Kronos the wily,

the youngest and most terrible of her children, who hated the most his vigorous father.

After she bore the Kyclopes who had overweening hearts:

Brontes and Steropes and the strong-minded Arges, 140

who gave Zeus the thunder and made the thunderbolt.

In everything else they were like the gods,

but one eye only was set in the middle of their foreheads

and they were surnamed "Kyclopes" (orb-eyed)

because one circular eye was set in their foreheads. 145

Strength, force, and scheming animated their deeds.

And again, three other sons were born of the Gaia and Ouranos,

great and mighty, not renowned,*

Kottos, Briareos, and Gyes: magnificent children.

From their shoulders one hundred arms quickly moved, 150

unapproachable; each had fifty heads

which arose from their strong shoulders, and in their strong limbs

and from their great shape they had terrible strength.

As many are the children that were born of Gaia and Ouranos

and of them the most fearful, were hated by their own father at the first. 155

As soon as each one was born

he hid him in the abyss, and he did not raise them into the light.

12   Metaphrasis: Dimitrios Kiriakopoulos

Γαίης ἐν κευθμῶνι, κακῷ δ' ἐπετέρπετο ἔργῳ

Οὐρανός. ἢ δ' ἐντὸς στοναχίζετο Γαῖα πελώρη

στεινομένη· δολίην δὲ κακήν τ' ἐφράσσατο τέχνην.   160

Αἶψα δὲ ποιήσασα γένος πολιοῦ ἀδάμαντος

τεῦξε μέγα δρέπανον καὶ ἐπέφραδε παισὶ φίλοισιν·

εἶπε δὲ θαρσύνουσα, φίλον τετιημένη ἦτορ·

«Παῖδες ἐμοὶ καὶ πατρὸς ἀτασθάλου, αἴ κ' ἐθέλητε

πείθεσθαι, πατρός κε κακὴν τισαίμεθα λώβην   165

ὑμετέρου· πρότερος γὰρ ἀεικέα μήσατο ἔργα.»

Ὣς φάτο· τοὺς δ' ἄρα πάντας ἕλεν δέος, οὐδέ τις αὐτῶν

φθέγξατο. Θαρσήσας δὲ μέγας Κρόνος ἀγκυλομήτης

ἂψ αὖτις μύθοισι προσηύδα μητέρα κεδνήν·

«Μῆτερ, ἐγώ κεν τοῦτό γ' ὑποσχόμενος τελέσαιμι   170

ἔργον, ἐπεὶ πατρός γε δυσωνύμου οὐκ ἀλεγίζω

ἡμετέρου· πρότερος γὰρ ἀεικέα μήσατο ἔργα».

Ὣς φάτο· γήθησεν δὲ μέγα φρεσὶ Γαῖα πελώρη·

Εἷσε δέ μιν κρύψασα λόχῳ· ἐνέθηκε δὲ χερσὶν

ἅρπην καρχαρόδοντα· δόλον δ' ὑπεθήκατο πάντα.   175

Ἦλθε δὲ νύκτ' ἐπάγων μέγας Οὐρανός, ἀμφὶ δὲ Γαίῃ

ἱμείρων φιλότητος ἐπέσχετο καί ῥ' ἐτανύσθη

πάντῃ· ὃ δ' ἐκ λοχεοῖο πάις ὠρέξατο χειρὶ

σκαιῇ, δεξιτερῇ δὲ πελώριον ἔλλαβεν ἅρπην

μακρὴν καρχαρόδοντα, φίλου δ' ἀπὸ μήδεα πατρὸς   180

ἐσσυμένως ἤμησε, πάλιν δ' ἔρριψε φέρεσθαι

ἐξοπίσω· τὰ μὲν οὔ τι ἐτώσια ἔκφυγε χειρός·

ὅσσαι γὰρ ῥαθάμιγγες ἀπέσσυθεν αἱματόεσσαι,

πάσας δέξατο Γαῖα· περιπλομένων δ' ἐνιαυτῶν

Ouranos rejoiced in his evil work,

but enormous Gaia, being distressed, groaned inside her

and she in turn planned a treacherous and cunning evil. 160

Quickly, she made the element of bright adamantite

and carved an enormous pruning-hook• and she said to her dear children,

encouraging them with sorrow in her dear heart,

"My children, children of a presumptuous father,

if you want be persuaded to punish your father's terrible misdeeds, 165

because first he did plan to do shameful things."

That is what she said, and at once fear seized them all

and none of them uttered a word. But great Kronos the wily,

with good courage answered his diligent mother,

"Mother, I promise to do this work, 170

for I don't care for a father bearing an ill name

because first he did plan to do shameful things."

So he said, and gigantic Gaia rejoiced in her heart.

Then she hid him in ambush and set in his hands

the sharp pruning-hook and revealed to him the whole guile. 175

The great Ouranos came, bringing the night,

and with desire for love, he did spread himself full upon her.

Then, from the ambush, his son stretched out and grabbed him with his left hand;

with his right he took the huge, long, sharp pruning-hook

and furiously he reaped off his father's genitals 180

and threw them behind him.

They did not, though, fall fruitlessly out of his hand—

for of the drops of blood that fell, all were received by Gaia

and in the fullness of time she bore the mighty Erinyes

14   Metaphrasis: Dimitrios Kiriakopoulos

γείνατ᾽ Ἐρινῦς τε κρατερὰς μεγάλους τε Γίγαντας,   185
τεύχεσι λαμπομένους, δολίχ᾽ ἔγχεα χερσὶν ἔχοντας,
Νύμφας θ᾽, ἃς Μελίας καλέουσ᾽ ἐπ᾽ ἀπείρονα γαῖαν.
Μήδεα δ᾽ ὡς τὸ πρῶτον ἀποτμήξας ἀδάμαντι
κάββαλ᾽ ἀπ᾽ ἠπείροιο πολυκλύστῳ ἐνὶ πόντῳ,
ὣς φέρετ᾽ ἂμ πέλαγος πουλὺν χρόνον, ἀμφὶ δὲ λευκὸς   190
ἀφρὸς ἀπ᾽ ἀθανάτου χροὸς ὤρνυτο· τῷ δ᾽ ἔνι κούρη
ἐθρέφθη· πρῶτον δὲ Κυθήροισιν ζαθέοισιν
ἔπλητ᾽, ἔνθεν ἔπειτα περίρρυτον ἵκετο Κύπρον.
Ἐκ δ᾽ ἔβη αἰδοίη καλὴ θεός, ἀμφὶ δὲ ποίη
ποσσὶν ὕπο ῥαδινοῖσιν ἀέξετο· τὴν δ᾽ Ἀφροδίτην   195
[ἀφρογενέα τε θεὰν καὶ ἐυστέφανον Κυθέρειαν]
κικλήσκουσι θεοί τε καὶ ἀνέρες, οὕνεκ᾽ ἐν ἀφρῷ
θρέφθη· ἀτὰρ Κυθέρειαν, ὅτι προσέκυρσε Κυθήροις·
[Κυπρογενέα δ᾽, ὅτι γέντο πολυκλύστῳ ἐνὶ Κύπρῳ·
ἠδὲ φιλομμηδέα, ὅτι μηδέων ἐξεφαάνθη.]   200
Τῇ δ᾽ Ἔρος ὡμάρτησε καὶ Ἵμερος ἕσπετο καλὸς
γεινομένῃ τὰ πρῶτα θεῶν τ᾽ ἐς φῦλον ἰούσῃ.
Ταύτην δ᾽ ἐξ ἀρχῆς τιμὴν ἔχει ἠδὲ λέλογχε
μοῖραν ἐν ἀνθρώποισι καὶ ἀθανάτοισι θεοῖσι,
Παρθενίους τ᾽ ὀάρους μειδήματά τ᾽ ἐξαπάτας τε   205
τέρψιν τε γλυκερὴν φιλότητά τε μειλιχίην τε.
Τοὺς δὲ πατὴρ Τιτῆνας ἐπίκλησιν καλέεσκε
παῖδας νεικείων μέγας Οὐρανός, οὓς τέκεν αὐτός·
φάσκε δὲ τιταίνοντας ἀτασθαλίῃ μέγα ῥέξαι
ἔργον, τοῖο δ᾽ ἔπειτα τίσιν μετόπισθεν ἔσεσθαι.   210
Νὺξ δ᾽ ἔτεκεν στυγερόν τε Μόρον καὶ Κῆρα μέλαιναν

and the great Gigantes with the shining armor, 185
holding long spears in their hands,
and the Nymphs also, whom they call Meliai all over the endless Gaia.
As soon as Kronos had cut off the genitals with the adamantite
and overthrew them from the land into the much-dashing open sea,
they were swept away for a long time over the high sea 190
and around that immortal flesh foam stirred up, and in it a maiden grew.
First she approached sacred Kythera
and from that point she came to sea-girt Kypros
and came forth a respectful and lovely goddess,
while around and beneath her slender feet, khloe sprung up. 195
"Aphrodite," call her the gods and humans,
the foam-born goddess and well-crowned Kytherea
because she was reared in foam and Kytherea because she arrived at Kythera
and Kyprogenes because she was born in billowy Kypros by the sea.
But also Philomedea because she sprung from the medea (genitals). 200
And Eros and Imeros accompanied her
when she was born, and at first followed her as she went into the race of gods.
This honor she has from the beginning and this is her destiny,
by the will of the gods: amongst the men and the immortals,
the love whisperings, the smiles, the deceits, 205
the pleasure and the sweet and gentle love.
The other children, whom he begot himself,
great Ouranos in anger called them Titanes (strainers),
for he said that they strained and committed big and presumptuous sin
and that punishment for it would come afterwards. 210
And Nyx (night) bore hateful Moros (doom) and black Keres (cruel death)*

καὶ Θάνατον, τέκε δ᾽ Ὕπνον, ἔτικτε δὲ φῦλον Ὀνείρων·

— οὔ τινι κοιμηθεῖσα θεὰ τέκε Νὺξ ἐρεβεννή, —

δεύτερον αὖ Μῶμον καὶ Ὀιζὺν ἀλγινόεσσαν

Ἑσπερίδας θ᾽, ἧς μῆλα πέρην κλυτοῦ Ὠκεανοῖο   215

χρύσεα καλὰ μέλουσι φέροντά τε δένδρεα καρπόν.

Καὶ Μοίρας καὶ Κῆρας ἐγείνατο νηλεοποίνους,

[Κλωθώ τε Λάχεσίν τε καὶ Ἄτροπον, αἵτε βροτοῖσι

γεινομένοισι διδοῦσιν ἔχειν ἀγαθόν τε κακόν τε,]

αἵτ᾽ ἀνδρῶν τε θεῶν τε παραιβασίας ἐφέπουσιν·   220

οὐδέ ποτε λήγουσι θεαὶ δεινοῖο χόλοιο,

πρίν γ᾽ ἀπὸ τῷ δώωσι κακὴν ὄπιν, ὅς τις ἁμάρτῃ.

Τίκτε δὲ καὶ Νέμεσιν, πῆμα θνητοῖσι βροτοῖσι,

Νὺξ ὀλοή· μετὰ τὴν δ᾽ Ἀπάτην τέκε καὶ Φιλότητα

Γῆράς τ᾽ οὐλόμενον, καὶ Ἔριν τέκε καρτερόθυμον.   225

Αὐτὰρ Ἔρις στυγερὴ τέκε μὲν Πόνον ἀλγινόεντα

Λήθην τε Λιμόν τε καὶ Ἄλγεα δακρυόεντα

Ὑσμίνας τε Μάχας τε Φόνους τ᾽ Ἀνδροκτασίας τε

Νείκεά τε ψευδέας τε Λόγους Ἀμφιλλογίας τε

Δυσνομίην τ᾽ Ἄάτην τε, συνήθεας ἀλλήλῃσιν,   230

Ὅρκον θ᾽, ὃς δὴ πλεῖστον ἐπιχθονίους ἀνθρώπους

πημαίνει, ὅτε κέν τις ἑκὼν ἐπίορκον ὀμόσσῃ.

Νηρέα δ᾽ ἀψευδέα καὶ ἀληθέα γείνατο Πόντος,

πρεσβύτατον παίδων· αὐτὰρ καλέουσι γέροντα,

οὕνεκα νημερτής τε καὶ ἤπιος, οὐδὲ θεμιστέων   235

λήθεται, ἀλλὰ δίκαια καὶ ἤπια δήνεα οἶδεν·

αὖτις δ᾽ αὖ Θαύμαντα μέγαν καὶ ἀγήνορα Φόρκυν

Γαίῃ μισγόμενος καὶ Κητὼ καλλιπάρηον

and Thanatos (death), and she also bore Hypnos (sleep)

and the tribe of Onoiroi (dreams) and again dark Night,

without laying with anyone, bore Momos (blame) and painful Oizys (woe)

and Hesperides, who guard the beautiful golden apples 215

and the bearing fruit trees across the famous ocean.*

She also gave birth to Moirai (fates) and Keres (death fates), the ruthless punishers,

and Klotho (spinning) and Lakhesis (measuring) and Atropos (cutting the thread of life),

who give to mortals at their birth both good and evil to have

and they pursue the deviations of men and the gods. 220

And these goddesses never cease from their dire anger

before they give hard punishment to the sinner.

Also, fatal Nyx bore Nemesis (envy), calamity of mortal men,

and after her, Apate (deceit) and Philotis (friendship),

the destructive Geras (age), and the stout-hearted Eris (strife). 225

Then, hateful Eris bore painful Ponos (pain) and Lethe (forgetfulness)

and Limos (famine) and the fearful Algae (grief).

Fighting, battles, murders, manslaughter,

quarrels, lying words, disputes, lawlessness,

and judicial blindness, all of one nature 230

and oath who most troubles men upon Earth,

when anyone purposely swears falsely.

And Pontos (sea) begot Nereus, the eldest of his children,

who is sincere and truthful.

People call him "old man" because he is infallible and gentle 235

and does not forget the custom established and he knows righteous and kindly plans.

And yet again, Pontos, having intercourse with Gaia,

begot great Thaumas and heroic Phorkys

18   Metaphrasis: Dimitrios Kiriakopoulos

Εὐρυβίην τ' ἀδάμαντος ἐνὶ φρεσὶ θυμὸν ἔχουσαν.

Νηρῆος δ' ἐγένοντο μεγήρατα τέκνα θεάων   240

πόντῳ ἐν ἀτρυγέτῳ καὶ Δωρίδος ἠυκόμοιο,

κούρης Ὠκεανοῖο, τελήεντος ποταμοῖο,

Πλωτώ τ' Εὐκράντη τε Σαώ τ' Ἀμφιτρίτη τε

Εὐδώρη τε Θέτις τε Γαλήνη τε Γλαύκη τε

Κυμοθόη Σπειώ τε Θόη θ' Ἁλίη τ' ἐρόεσσα   245

Πασιθέη τ' Ἐρατώ τε καὶ Εὐνίκη ῥοδόπηχυς

καὶ Μελίτη χαρίεσσα καὶ Εὐλιμένη καὶ Ἀγαυὴ

Δωτώ τε Πρωτώ τε Φέρουσά τε Δυναμένη τε

Νησαίη τε καὶ Ἀκταίη καὶ Πρωτομέδεια

Δωρὶς καὶ Πανόπεια καὶ εὐειδὴς Γαλάτεια   250

Ἱπποθόη τ' ἐρόεσσα καὶ Ἱππονόη ῥοδόπηχυς

Κυμοδόκη θ', ἣ κύματ' ἐν ἠεροειδέι πόντῳ

πνοιάς τε ζαέων ἀνέμων σὺν Κυματολήγῃ

ῥεῖα πρηΰνει καὶ ἐυσφύρῳ Ἀμφιτρίτῃ,

Κυμώ τ' Ἠιόνη τε ἐυστέφανός θ' Ἁλιμήδη   255

Γλαυκονόμη τε φιλομμειδὴς καὶ Ποντοπόρεια

Ληαγόρη τε καὶ Εὐαγόρη καὶ Λαομέδεια

Πουλυνόη τε καὶ Αὐτονόη καὶ Λυσιάνασσα

[Εὐάρνη τε φυήν τ' ἐρατὴ καὶ εἶδος ἄμωμος]

καὶ Ψαμάθη χαρίεσσα δέμας δίη τε Μενίππη   260

Νησώ τ' Εὐπόμπη τε Θεμιστώ τε Προνόη τε

Νημερτής θ', ἣ πατρὸς ἔχει νόον ἀθανάτοιο.

Αὗται μὲν Νηρῆος ἀμύμονος ἐξεγένοντο

κοῦραι πεντήκοντα, ἀμύμονα ἔργα ἰδυῖαι.

Θαύμας δ' Ὠκεανοῖο βαθυρρείταο θύγατρα   265

and beautiful-cheeked Keto and Eurybia who has an adamantine soul in her chest.
And of Nereus and fair-haired Doris, 240
daughter of Okeanos, the perfect river,
were born lovely children of gods in the unfruitful sea:
Ploto, Eucrante, Sao, and Amphitrite,
Eudora, Thetis, Galene, and Glauke,
Kymothoe, Speo, Thoe, and charming Alia, 245
Pasithea, Erato, and rosy-armed Eunike,
and gracious Melite and Eulimene and Agave,
Doto, Proto, Pherousa, and Dynamene,
Nisaia, Actaia, and Protomedeia,
Doris, Panopea, and beautiful Galatea 250
and lovely Hippothoe, and rosy-armed Hipponoe,
Kymodoke, who with Kymatolege easily calms the waves
and the blasts of raging winds upon the misty sea,
and beautiful-ankled Amphitrite,
Kymo, Eione, and well-crowned Alimede, 255
Glauconome the always smiling, and Pontoporea,
Leagore, Euagore, and Laomedea,
Polynoe, Autonoe, and Lysianassa,
Euarne with lovely stature and blameless figure,
Psamathe of charming shape, and divine Mennipe, 260
Neso, Eupompe, Themisto, and Pronoe,
and Nemertes who has the mind of her immortal father.
These fifty daughters were born from noble Nereus,
who knows to do excellent things.
Thaumas married Electra, the daughter of deep-flowing Okeanos, 265

20   Metaphrasis: Dimitrios Kiriakopoulos

ἠγάγετ' Ἠλέκτρην· ἣ δ' ὠκεῖαν τέκεν Ἶριν

ἠυκόμους θ' Ἁρπυίας Ἀελλώ τ' Ὠκυπέτην τε,

αἵ ῥ' ἀνέμων πνοιῇσι καὶ οἰωνοῖς ἅμ' ἕπονται

ὠκείης πτερύγεσσι· μεταχρόνιαι γὰρ ἴαλλον.

Φόρκυϊ δ' αὖ Κητὼ Γραίας τέκε καλλιπαρῄους   270

ἐκ γενετῆς πολιάς, τὰς δὴ Γραίας καλέουσιν

ἀθάνατοί τε θεοὶ χαμαὶ ἐρχόμενοί τ' ἄνθρωποι,

Πεμφρηδώ τ' ἐύπεπλον Ἐνυώ τε κροκόπεπλον,

Γοργούς θ', αἵ ναίουσι πέρην κλυτοῦ Ὠκεανοῖο

ἐσχατιῇ πρὸς Νυκτός, ἵν' Ἑσπερίδες λιγύφωνοι,   275

Σθεννώ τ' Εὐρυάλη τε Μέδουσά τε λυγρὰ παθοῦσα.

Ἣ μὲν ἔην θνητή, αἱ δ' ἀθάνατοι καὶ ἀγήρῳ,

αἱ δύο· τῇ δὲ μιῇ παρελέξατο Κυανοχαίτης

ἐν μαλακῷ λειμῶνι καὶ ἄνθεσιν εἰαρινοῖσιν.

Τῆς δ' ὅτε δὴ Περσεὺς κεφαλὴν ἀπεδειροτόμησεν,   280

ἔκθορε Χρυσάωρ τε μέγας καὶ Πήγασος ἵππος.

Τῷ μὲν ἐπώνυμον ἦεν, ὅτ' Ὠκεανοῦ περὶ πηγὰς

γένθ', ὃ δ' ἄορ χρύσειον ἔχων μετὰ χερσὶ φίλῃσιν.

Χὠ μὲν ἀποπτάμενος προλιπὼν χθόνα, μητέρα μήλων,

ἵκετ' ἐς ἀθανάτους· Ζηνὸς δ' ἐν δώμασι ναίει   285

βροντήν τε στεροπήν τε φέρων Διὶ μητιόεντι.

Χρυσάωρ δ' ἔτεκεν τρικέφαλον Γηρυονῆα

μιχθεὶς Καλλιρόῃ κούρῃ κλυτοῦ Ὠκεανοῖο.

Τὸν μὲν ἄρ' ἐξενάριξε βίη Ἡρακληείη

βουσὶ παρ' εἰλιπόδεσσι περιρρύτῳ εἰν Ἐρυθείῃ   290

ἤματι τῷ ὅτε περ βοῦς ἤλασεν εὐρυμετώπους

Τίρυνθ' εἰς ἱερὴν διαβὰς πόρον Ὠκεανοῖο

who bore swift Iris and the fair-haired Harpies,
Aello (storm-swift) and Okypetes (swift-flier),
who follow the blasts of the wind and the birds,
flying high in the sky on their sharp wings.
And Kyto bore to Phorkys the fair-cheeked Graiai, 270
gray-haired from their birth, so Graiai are named
from immortal gods and humans who come to earth,
Pamphedo the well and Enyo the crocus-gladed
and Gorgons who dwell on the other side of the famous ocean
at the edge of the night where the sweet-voiced Hesperides are, 275
Stheno, Euryale, and Medusa who suffered woefully,
the only mortal, but the other two immortal and undecaying.
With her lay the azure-haired one (Poseidon)
in a soft meadow with spring flowers.
When Perseus beheaded Medusa, 280
from her head leaped out the great Khrysaor and the horse Pegasos,
who is so called for he was born near the springs of the ocean
and the other because he held a golden sword in his dear hands.
Pegasos flew off and left Gaia, the mother of sheep,
and came to the immortals. He dwells in the house of Zeus, 285
bringing to the all-wise Zeus thunder and lightning.
Khrysaor got united with Kallirhoe, daughter of famous Okeanos,
and begot three-headed Geryones,
who got killed by the force of Herakles
in the sea-girt Erythea by his reeling oxen 290
on this day, when he drove the broad-fronted oxen to holy Tiryns,
passing the strait of the ocean,

22 Metaphrasis: Dimitrios Kiriakopoulos

Ὄρθον τε κτείνας καὶ βουκόλον Εὐρυτίωνα
σταθμῷ ἐν ἠερόεντι πέρην κλυτοῦ Ὠκεανοῖο.
Ἥ δ᾽ ἔτεκ᾽ ἄλλο πέλωρον ἀμήχανον, οὐδὲν ἐοικὸς 295
θνητοῖς ἀνθρώποις οὐδ᾽ ἀθανάτοισι θεοῖσιν,
ἐν σπῆι ἔνι γλαφυρῷ θείην κρατερόφρον᾽ Ἔχιδναν,
ἥμισυ μὲν νύμφην ἑλικώπιδα καλλιπάρῃον,
ἥμισυ δ᾽ αὖτε πέλωρον ὄφιν δεινόν τε μέγαν τε
αἰόλον ὠμηστὴν ζαθέης ὑπὸ κεύθεσι γαίης. 300
Ἔνθα δέ οἱ σπέος ἐστὶ κάτω κοίλῃ ὑπὸ πέτρῃ
τηλοῦ ἀπ᾽ ἀθανάτων τε θεῶν θνητῶν τ᾽ ἀνθρώπων·
ἔνθ᾽ ἄρα οἱ δάσσαντο θεοὶ κλυτὰ δώματα ναίειν.
Ἥ δ᾽ ἔρυτ᾽ εἰν Ἀρίμοισιν ὑπὸ χθόνα λυγρὴ Ἔχιδνα,
ἀθάνατος νύμφη καὶ ἀγήραος ἤματα πάντα. 305
Τῇ δὲ Τυφάονά φασι μιγήμεναι ἐν φιλότητι
δεινόν θ᾽ ὑβριστήν τ᾽ ἄνομόν θ᾽ ἑλικώπιδι κούρῃ·
ἣ δ᾽ ὑποκυσαμένη τέκετο κρατερόφρονα τέκνα.
Ὄρθον μὲν πρῶτον κύνα γείνατο Γηρυονῆι·
δεύτερον αὖτις ἔτικτεν ἀμήχανον, οὔ τι φατειὸν 310
Κέρβερον ὠμηστήν, Ἀίδεω κύνα χαλκεόφωνον,
πεντηκοντακέφαλον, ἀναιδέα τε κρατερόν τε·
τὸ τρίτον Ὕδρην αὖτις ἐγείνατο λυγρὰ ἰδυῖαν
Λερναίην, ἣν θρέψε θεὰ λευκώλενος Ἥρη
ἄπλητον κοτέουσα βίῃ Ἡρακληείῃ. 315
Καὶ τὴν μὲν Διὸς υἱὸς ἐνήρατο νηλέι χαλκῷ
Ἀμφιτρυωνιάδης σὺν ἀρηιφίλῳ Ἰολάῳ
Ἡρακλέης βουλῇσιν Ἀθηναίης ἀγελείης.
Ἥ δὲ Χίμαιραν ἔτικτε πνέουσαν ἀμαιμάκετον πῦρ,

killing also Orthos and the herdsman Eurytion

in the murky stable, far across the renowned ocean.

And Kallirhoe also bore another extraordinary monster, 295

who has nothing in common with mortal men and the immortal gods,

in a hollow cave, sent by the gods, the stout-hearted Ekhidna,

who is half a Nymph with quick, glancing eyes and fair cheeks,

and the other half a gigantic snake, fearful and great, quick-moving,

eating raw flesh in the depths of divine Gaia. 300

That is where she has a cave, deep under a hollow rock,

far from the immortal gods and the mortal humans.

There then, the gods did appoint her splendid halls to dwell.

The baneful Ekhidna is dragged to guard Arima

under the earth, deathless Nymph and undecaying at all times. 305

They say that Typhaon the terrible, violent and lawless,

was joined in love to her, the quick-glancing maid,

so she conceived and bore stout-hearted children.

First she bore Orthos, the dog of Geryones,

and then again the second one, untamed and unspeakable, 310

Kerberos, the raw flesh-eater, the clear and strong-voiced dog of Hades,

the fifty-headed, relentless and cruel.

And again, she bore a third, Hydra of Lerna, the malicious,

whom the Goddess, the white-armed Hera reared,

being angry beyond limit with the strength of Herakles. 315

And her, the son of Zeus, Herakles, of the house of Amphitrion

together with warlike Iolaos, slew with ruthless steel

and the will of Athena, the spoil-driver.

She (Ekhidna) also gave birth to Khimaira, who breathed irresistible fire,

24 Metaphrasis: Dimitrios Kiriakopoulos

δεινήν τε μεγάλην τε ποδώκεά τε κρατερήν τε· 320

Τῆς δ' ἦν τρεῖς κεφαλαί· μία μὲν χαροποῖο λέοντος,

ἣ δὲ χιμαίρης, ἣ δ' ὄφιος, κρατεροῖο δράκοντος,

[πρόσθε λέων, ὄπιθεν δὲ δράκων, μέσση δὲ χίμαιρα,

δεινὸν ἀποπνείουσα πυρὸς μένος αἰθομένοιο.]

Τὴν μὲν Πήγασος εἷλε καὶ ἐσθλὸς Βελλεροφόντης. 325

Ἣ δ' ἄρα Φῖκ' ὀλοὴν τέκε Καδμείοισιν ὄλεθρον

Ὄρθῳ ὑποδμηθεῖσα Νεμειαῖόν τε λέοντα,

τόν ῥ' Ἥρη θρέψασα Διὸς κυδρὴ παράκοιτις

γουνοῖσιν κατένασσε Νεμείης, πῆμ' ἀνθρώποις.

Ἔνθ' ἄρ' ὃ οἰκείων ἐλεφαίρετο φῦλ' ἀνθρώπων, 330

κοιρανέων Τρητοῖο Νεμείης ἠδ' Ἀπέσαντος·

ἀλλά ἑ ἲς ἐδάμασσε βίης Ἡρακληείης.

Κητὼ δ' ὁπλότατον Φόρκυι φιλότητι μιγεῖσα

γείνατο δεινὸν ὄφιν, ὅς ἐρεμνῆς κεύθεσι γαίης

σπείρησιν μεγάλοις παγχρύσεα μῆλα φυλάσσει. 335

Τοῦτο μὲν ἐκ Κητοῦς καὶ Φόρκυνος γένος ἐστίν.

Τηθὺς δ' Ὠκεανῷ Ποταμοὺς τέκε δινήεντας,

Νεῖλόν τ' Ἀλφειόν τε καὶ Ἠριδανὸν βαθυδίνην

Στρυμόνα Μαίανδρόν τε καὶ Ἴστρον καλλιρέεθρον

Φᾶσίν τε Ῥῆσόν τ' Ἀχελωϊόν τ' ἀργυροδίνην 340

Νέσσον τε Ῥοδίον θ' Ἁλιάκμονά θ' Ἑπτάπορόν τε

Γρήνικόν τε καὶ Αἴσηπον θεῖόν τε Σιμοῦντα

Πηνειόν τε καὶ Ἕρμον εὐρρείτην τε Κάικον

Σαγγάριόν τε μέγαν Λάδωνά τε Παρθένιόν τε

Εὔηνόν τε καὶ Ἄρδησκον θεῖόν τε Σκάμανδρον. 345

Τίκτε δὲ θυγατέρων ἱερὸν γένος, αἳ κατὰ γαῖαν

fearful and great and swift-footed and mighty, 320
who had three heads, one of a bright-eyed lion,
one of a goat, and one of a stout dragon
(lion at the front, dragon in the hinder part and goat in the middle,
blowing fearful blasts of blazing fire).
And her (Khimaira) did Pegasos and brave Bellerophon kill. 325
But Ekhidna, being subdued to Orthos,
brought forth the deadly sphinx, plague of the Kadmeans
and the lion of Nemea, which Hera, the glorious wife of Zeus, brought up
and settled him on the hills of Nemea, a suffering for humans.
From there, he destroyed the domestic tribes of people 330
and had power over Tretos of Nemea and Apesas.
Yet the force of strong Herakles tamed him (the lion of Nemea).
When Keto joined in love to Phorkys, she bore her youngest child,
an awful snake who guards in the dark depths
at the end of the earth all the gold apples. 335
This is the offspring of Keto and Phorkys.
And Tethys bore to Okeanos eddying Rivers,
Nilos and Alpheios and deep-swirling Eridanos,
Strymon and Meandros and the fair-streamed Istros,
and Phasis and Phesos and the silver-whirled Akheloos, 340
Rhodios and Haliakmon and Heptaporos,
Granikos and Aisepos and holy Simois,
Peneos, Hermos, and fair-flowing Kaikos,
great Sangarios, Ladon, Parthenios,
and Euenos, Ardeskos, and divine Skamandros. 345
Also she bore the holy race of daughters, who with the lord Apollo

ἄνδρας κουρίζουσι σὺν Ἀπόλλωνι ἄνακτι

καὶ Ποταμοῖς, ταύτην δὲ Διὸς πάρα μοῖραν ἔχουσι,

Πειθώ τ' Ἀδμήτη τε Ἰάνθη τ' Ἠλέκτρη τε

Δωρίς τε Πρυμνώ τε καὶ Οὐρανίη θεοειδὴς 350

Ἱππώ τε Κλυμένη τε ῾Ρόδειά τε Καλλιρόη τε

Ζευξώ τε Κλυτίη τε Ἰδυῖά τε Πασιθόη τε

Πληξαύρη τε Γαλαξαύρη τ' ἐρατή τε Διώνη

Μηλόβοσίς τε Φόη τε καὶ εὐειδὴς Πολυδώρη

Κερκηίς τε φυὴν ἐρατὴ Πλουτώ τε βοῶπις 355

Περσηίς τ' Ἰάνειρά τ' Ἀκάστη τε Ξάνθη τε

Πετραίη τ' ἐρόεσσα Μενεσθώ τ' Εὐρώπη τε

Μῆτίς τ' Εὐρυνόμη τε Τελεστώ τε κροκόπεπλος

Χρυσηίς τ' Ἀσίη τε καὶ ἱμερόεσσα Καλυψὼ

Εὐδώρη τε Τύχη τε καὶ Ἀμφιρὼ Ὠκυρόη τε 360

καὶ Στύξ, ἢ δή σφεων προφερεστάτη ἐστὶν ἁπασέων.

Αὗται δ' Ὠκεανοῦ καὶ Τηθύος ἐξεγένοντο

πρεσβύταται κοῦραι· πολλαί γε μέν εἰσι καὶ ἄλλαι.

Τρὶς γὰρ χίλιαί εἰσι τανύσφυροι Ὠκεανῖναι,

αἵ ῥα πολυσπερέες γαῖαν καὶ βένθεα λίμνης 365

πάντη ὁμῶς ἐφέπουσι, θεάων ἀγλαὰ τέκνα.

Τόσσοι δ' αὖθ' ἕτεροι ποταμοὶ καναχηδὰ ῥέοντες,

υἱέες Ὠκεανοῦ, τοὺς γείνατο πότνια Τηθύς·

τῶν ὄνομ' ἀργαλέον πάντων βροτὸν ἀνέρ' ἐνισπεῖν,

Οἳ δὲ ἕκαστοι ἴσασιν, ὅσοι περιναιετάωσιν. 370

Θεία δ' Ἠέλιόν τε μέγαν λαμπράν τε Σελήνην

Ἠῶ θ', ἣ πάντεσσιν ἐπιχθονίοισι φαείνει

ἀθανάτοις τε θεοῖσι, τοὶ οὐρανὸν εὐρὺν ἔχουσι,

and the Rivers bring up on earth man from boyhood.
This was their fate appointed by Zeus.
Peitho, Admete, and Ianthe and Elektra,
Doris, Prymno, and divine-formed Ourania, 350
Hippo and Kleme, Rodhea and Kallirhoe,
Zeuxo, Klytia, and Idyia and Pasithoe,
Plexaure, Galaxaure, and lovely Dione,
Melobosis, Thoe, and well-shaped Polydore,
lovely-statured Kerkeis and the large, full-eyed Plouto, 355
Perseis, Ianeira, Akaste, Xanthe,
lovely Petraia, Menestho, and Europa,
Metis and Eurynome, crocus-veiled Telesto,
Khryseis and Asia, charming Kalypso,
Eudora, Tykhe and Amphiro, Okyrrhoe, 360
and Styx, who is the superior of them all.
These are the eldest daughters that sprung from Okeanos and Tethys,
but there are a lot more,
three thousand long-ankled Okeanides,
widely spread on the earth and depths of the lakes, 365
everywhere, with common pursuits, splendid children of the gods.
And again, as many rivers are there that flow with sharp, loud voice,
sons of Okeanos, whom bore Queen Tethys.
It is hard for a mortal man all these names to tell,
but they are known to people who dwell all around. 370
And Theia bore great Helios (sun) and bright Selene (moon)
and Eos (dawn), who brings the light to all the humans
and the immortal gods who possess the wide sky,

γείναθ' ὑποδμηθεῖσ' Ὑπερίονος ἐν φιλότητι.

Κρίῳ δ' Εὐρυβίη τέκεν ἐν φιλότητι μιγεῖσα 375

Ἀστραῖόν τε μέγαν Πάλλαντά τε δῖα θεάων

Πέρσην θ', ὃς καὶ πᾶσι μετέπρεπεν ἰδμοσύνησιν.

Ἀστραίῳ δ' Ἠὼς ἀνέμους τέκε καρτεροθύμους,

ἀργέστην Ζέφυρον Βορέην τ' αἰψηροκέλευθον

καὶ Νότον, ἐν φιλότητι θεὰ θεῷ εὐνηθεῖσα. 380

Τοὺς δὲ μέτ' ἀστέρα τίκτ' Ἠοσφόρον Ἠριγένεια

ἄστρα τε λαμπετόωντα, τά τ' οὐρανὸς ἐστεφάνωται.

Στὺξ δ' ἔτεκ' Ὠκεανοῦ θυγάτηρ Πάλλαντι μιγεῖσα

Ζῆλον καὶ Νίκην καλλίσφυρον ἐν μεγάροισιν·

καὶ Κράτος ἠδὲ Βίην ἀριδείκετα γείνατο τέκνα, 385

τῶν οὐκ ἔστ' ἀπάνευθε Διὸς δόμος, οὐδέ τις ἕδρη,

οὐδ' ὁδός, ὅππη μὴ κείνοις θεὸς ἡγεμονεύῃ,

ἀλλ' αἰεὶ πὰρ Ζηνὶ βαρυκτύπῳ ἑδριόωνται.

Ὣς γὰρ ἐβούλευσεν Στὺξ ἄφθιτος Ὠκεανίνη

ἤματι τῷ, ὅτε πάντας Ὀλύμπιος ἀστεροπητὴς 390

ἀθανάτους ἐκάλεσσε θεοὺς ἐς μακρὸν Ὄλυμπον,

εἶπε δ', ὅς ἂν μετὰ εἷο θεῶν Τιτῆσι μάχοιτο,

μή τιν' ἀπορραίσειν γεράων, τιμὴν δὲ ἕκαστον

ἑξέμεν, ἣν τὸ πάρος γε μετ' ἀθανάτοισι θεοῖσιν

Τὸν δ' ἔφαθ', ὅς τις ἄτιμος ὑπὸ Κρόνου ἠδ' ἀγέραστος, 395

τιμῆς καὶ γεράων ἐπιβησέμεν, ἥ θέμις ἐστίν.

Ἦλθε δ' ἄρα πρώτη Στὺξ ἄφθιτος Οὔλυμπόνδε

σὺν σφοῖσιν παίδεσσι φίλου διὰ μήδεα πατρός.

Τὴν δὲ Ζεὺς τίμησε, περισσὰ δὲ δῶρα ἔδωκεν.

Αὐτὴν μὲν γὰρ ἔθηκε θεῶν μέγαν ἔμμεναι ὅρκον, 400

when she had been subdued to Hyperion.

And Eurybia, divine goddess, joined in love to Krios 375

and bore great Astraios and Pallas and Perses

who was distinguished among all others in knowledge.

And Eos bore to Astraios the mighty winds,

Zephyros the north-west wind, Boreas the swift speeding

and Notos, when the goddess fell in love and she went to bed with the god. 380

And after them, Erigenia bore the star Eosphoros

and the shining stars with which the sky is crowned.

And Styx, the daughter of Okeanos, joined to Pallas and she bore in her palace

Zelos (jealousy) and the beautiful-ankled Niki.

Also, she brought forth Kratos (strength) and Via (force), most renowned children, 385

who have a house not far from Zeus, nor a seat,

nor a path, where the god cannot lead the way,

but always near Zeus the loud-thunderer sit.

So Styx, the imperishable daughter of Okeanos, in this manner

thought on that day when the Olympian lightener, 390

did call all the immortal gods to tall Olympos and said that

whoever of the gods would fight with him against the Titanes,

he would not strip him of his rights but each should have the honor

which he had formerly among the immortal gods

and he declared that he who was formerly without a gift of honor 395

and deprived of privileges as the custom is, he will advance with reward and prerogatives.

Then immortal Styx first came to Olympos with her children,

through the counsels of her dear father.

And Zeus, honored and prodigious gifts he gave her.

He appointed her waters to be the great oath of the gods 400

παῖδας δ' ἤματα πάντα ἕο μεταναιέτας εἶναι.

Ὣς δ' αὔτως πάντεσσι διαμπερές, ὥς περ ὑπέστη,

ἐξετέλεσσ'· αὐτὸς δὲ μέγα κρατεῖ ἠδὲ ἀνάσσει.

Φοίβη δ' αὖ Κοίου πολυήρατον ἦλθεν ἐς εὐνήν·

κυσαμένη δὴ ἔπειτα θεὰ θεοῦ ἐν φιλότητι 405

Λητὼ κυανόπεπλον ἐγείνατο, μείλιχον αἰεί,

ἤπιον ἀνθρώποισι καὶ ἀθανάτοισι θεοῖσιν.

μείλιχον ἐξ ἀρχῆς, ἀγανώτατον ἐντὸς Ὀλύμπου,

Γείνατο δ' Ἀστερίην εὐώνυμον, ἥν ποτε Πέρσης

ἠγάγετ' ἐς μέγα δῶμα φίλην κεκλῆσθαι ἄκοιτιν. 410

Ἥ δ' ὑποκυσαμένη Ἑκάτην τέκε, τὴν περὶ πάντων

Ζεὺς Κρονίδης τίμησε· πόρεν δέ οἱ ἀγλαὰ δῶρα,

μοῖραν ἔχειν γαίης τε καὶ ἀτρυγέτοιο θαλάσσης.

Ἥ δὲ καὶ ἀστερόεντος ἀπ' οὐρανοῦ ἔμμορε τιμῆς

ἀθανάτοις τε θεοῖσι τετιμένη ἐστὶ μάλιστα. 415

Καὶ γὰρ νῦν, ὅτε πού τις ἐπιχθονίων ἀνθρώπων

ἔρδων ἱερὰ καλὰ κατὰ νόμον ἱλάσκηται,

κικλῄσκει Ἑκάτην· πολλή τέ οἱ ἕσπετο τιμὴ

ῥεῖα μάλ', ᾧ πρόφρων γε θεὰ ὑποδέξεται εὐχάς,

καί τέ οἱ ὄλβον ὀπάζει, ἐπεὶ δύναμίς γε πάρεστιν. 420

Ὅσσοι γὰρ Γαίης τε καὶ Οὐρανοῦ ἐξεγένοντο

καὶ τιμὴν ἔλαχον, τούτων ἔχει αἶσαν ἁπάντων.

Οὐδέ τί μιν Κρονίδης ἐβιήσατο οὐδέ τ' ἀπηύρα,

ὅσσ' ἔλαχεν Τιτῆσι μετὰ προτέροισι θεοῖσιν,

ἀλλ' ἔχει, ὡς τὸ πρῶτον ἀπ' ἀρχῆς ἔπλετο δασμός, 425

οὐδ', ὅτι μουνογενής, ἧσσον θεὰ ἔμμορε τιμῆς,

καὶ γέρας ἐν γαίῃ τε καὶ οὐρανῷ ἠδὲ θαλάσσῃ·

and her children to live with him always.

As he promised to all what throughout he perfectly did,

so he, himself with power, reigns and rules.

And again, Phoebe went to bed with much loved Koeos,

then the goddess, through the love of the god 405

conceived and brought forth the dark blue-veiled Leto: always gentle,

kind to people and the immortal gods,

from the beginning mild and gentlest in all Olympos.

Then Phoebe brought forth the honored Asteria, whom Perses once

led to his great house to be called his dear wife. 410

And she (Asteria) bore Hekate, whom Kronides Zeus

honored above all. He did give her bright gifts

to have a share on the earth and the unfruitful sea.

She also received honors from the starry sky

and has been the most honored by the immortal gods. 415

For to this time, whenever any man on earth

offers auspicious sacrifices and is propitiated according to customs,

he calls upon Hekate. To him whose prayers

the goddess receives favorably, she easily gives in return very much honor,

followed by happiness because she has the power. 420

For as many as were born of Gaia and Ouranos

and received honors, they all shared a portion with her,

while Zeus never used force on her, nor took anything away

of all that was given to the Titanes and the first gods,

but she holds all that was given from the beginning: 425

privilege in earth and in sky and in sea.

Also, because she was the only begotten child,

32   Metaphrasis: Dimitrios Kiriakopoulos

ἀλλ' ἔτι καὶ πολὺ μᾶλλον, ἐπεὶ Ζεὺς τίεται αὐτήν.
Ὧι δ' ἐθέλει, μεγάλως παραγίγνεται ἠδ' ὀνίνησιν·
ἔν τε δίκῃ βασιλεῦσι παρ' αἰδοίοισι καθίζει,   430
ἔν τ' ἀγορῇ λαοῖσι μεταπρέπει, ὅν κ' ἐθέλῃσιν·
ἠδ' ὁπότ' ἐς πόλεμον φθεισήνορα θωρήσσωνται
ἀνέρες, ἔνθα θεὰ παραγίγνεται, οἷς κ' ἐθέλῃσι
νίκην προφρονέως ὀπάσαι καὶ κῦδος ὀρέξαι.
Ἐσθλὴ δ' αὖθ' ὁπότ' ἄνδρες ἀεθλεύωσιν ἀγῶνι,   435
ἔνθα θεὰ καὶ τοῖς παραγίγνεται ἠδ' ὀνίνησιν·
νικήσας δὲ βίῃ καὶ κάρτεϊ καλὸν ἄεθλον
ῥεῖα φέρει χαίρων τε, τοκεῦσι δὲ κῦδος ὀπάζει.
Ἐσθλὴ δ' ἱππήεσσι παρεστάμεν, οἷς κ' ἐθέλῃσιν.
Καὶ τοῖς, οἳ γλαυκὴν δυσπέμφελον ἐργάζονται,   440
εὔχονται δ' Ἑκάτῃ καὶ ἐρικτύπῳ Ἐννοσιγαίῳ,
ῥηιδίως ἄγρην κυδρὴ θεὸς ὤπασε πολλήν,
ῥεῖα δ' ἀφείλετο φαινομένην, ἐθέλουσά γε θυμῷ.
Ἐσθλὴ δ' ἐν σταθμοῖσι σὺν Ἑρμῇ ληίδ' ἀέξειν·
βουκολίας δ' ἀγέλας τε καὶ αἰπόλια πλατέ' αἰγῶν   445
ποίμνας τ' εἰροπόκων ὀίων, θυμῷ γ' ἐθέλουσα,
ἐξ ὀλίγων βριάει καὶ ἐκ πολλῶν μείονα θῆκεν.
Οὕτω τοι καὶ μουνογενὴς ἐκ μητρὸς ἐοῦσα
πᾶσι μετ' ἀθανάτοισι τετίμηται γεράεσσιν.
Θῆκε δέ μιν Κρονίδης κουροτρόφον, οἳ μετ' ἐκείνην   450
ὀφθαλμοῖσιν ἴδοντο φάος πολυδερκέος Ἠοῦς.
Οὕτως ἐξ ἀρχῆς κουροτρόφος, αἳ δέ τε τιμαί.
Ῥείη δὲ δμηθεῖσα Κρόνῳ τέκε φαίδιμα τέκνα,
Ἱστίην Δήμητρα καὶ Ἥρην χρυσοπέδιλον

she did not receive less honor, but much, much more
because Zeus honors her. Whom she wants,
she greatly assists and benefits. In the public assembly, 430
in judgment she sits by the worshipful kings
and whom she will favor is distinguished among the people.
When men arm themselves for the war that destroys men,
there the goddess comes to support and greatly gives victory
and hands out triumph to whom she wants. Good she is also, 435
when men contend at the games. There, too, the goddess attends and assists
and he who by might and strength gets the victory,
easily and with joy wins the beautiful prize and brings glory to his parents.
She is also good to stand by the horsemen, to whom she will.
And to those who work in the uncourteous and gleaming sea 440
and pray to Hekate and the loud-sounding earth-shaker,
the glorious goddess easily gives great catch
and easily, if her heart wishes, she takes the catch away as soon as seen.
She is good to the stables and, together with Hermes, she increases the stock.
If she will, she increases from few, or makes many to be less 445
the herds of cattle, the wide goat-herds,
and the flocks of wool-fleeced sheep.
So then, Albeit is her mother's only child;
she is honored and privileged amongst the immortals.
And Zeus made her nurse of young boys, who after that day 450
saw with their eyes the light of the much-seeing Dawn.
So, from the beginning, she is the nurse of the young and these are her honors.
Then Rhea, being submitted to Kronos, bore glorious children:
Hestia, Demeter, and gold-sandaled Hera,

34 Metaphrasis: Dimitrios Kiriakopoulos

ἴφθιμόν τ' Ἀίδην, ὃς ὑπὸ χθονὶ δώματα ναίει 455

νηλεὲς ἦτορ ἔχων, καὶ ἐρίκτυπον Ἐννοσίγαιον

Ζῆνά τε μητιόεντα, θεῶν πατέρ' ἠδὲ καὶ ἀνδρῶν,

τοῦ καὶ ὑπὸ βροντῆς πελεμίζεται εὐρεῖα χθών.

Καὶ τοὺς μὲν κατέπινε μέγας Κρόνος, ὥς τις ἕκαστος

νηδύος ἐξ ἱερῆς μητρὸς πρὸς γούναθ' ἵκοιτο, 460

τὰ φρονέων, ἵνα μή τις ἀγαυῶν Οὐρανιώνων

ἄλλος ἐν ἀθανάτοισιν ἔχοι βασιληίδα τιμήν.

Πεύθετο γὰρ Γαίης τε καὶ Οὐρανοῦ ἀστερόεντος,

οὕνεκά οἱ πέπρωτο ἑῷ ὑπὸ παιδὶ δαμῆναι

καὶ κρατερῷ περ ἐόντι — Διὸς μεγάλου διὰ βουλάς· — 465

τῷ ὅ γ' ἄρ' οὐκ ἀλαὸς σκοπιὴν ἔχεν, ἀλλὰ δοκεύων

παῖδας ἑοὺς κατέπινε· Ῥέην δ' ἔχε πένθος ἄλαστον.

Ἀλλ' ὅτε δὴ Δί' ἔμελλε θεῶν πατέρ' ἠδὲ καὶ ἀνδρῶν

τέξεσθαι, τότ' ἔπειτα φίλους λιτάνευε τοκῆας

τοὺς αὐτῆς, Γαῖάν τε καὶ Οὐρανὸν ἀστερόεντα, 470

μῆτιν συμφράσσασθαι, ὅπως λελάθοιτο τεκοῦσα

παῖδα φίλον, τείσαιτο δ' ἐρινῦς πατρὸς ἑοῖο

παίδων θ', οὓς κατέπινε μέγας Κρόνος ἀγκυλομήτης.

Οἳ δὲ θυγατρὶ φίλῃ μάλα μὲν κλύον ἠδ' ἐπίθοντο,

καί οἱ πεφραδέτην, ὅσα περ πέπρωτο γενέσθαι 475

ἀμφὶ Κρόνῳ βασιλῆι καὶ υἱέι καρτεροθύμῳ.

Πέμψαν δ' ἐς Λύκτον, Κρήτης ἐς πίονα δῆμον,

ὁππότ' ἄρ' ὁπλότατον παίδων τέξεσθαι ἔμελλε,

Ζῆνα μέγαν· τὸν μέν οἱ ἐδέξατο Γαῖα πελώρη

Κρήτῃ ἐν εὐρείῃ τραφέμεν ἀτιταλλέμεναί τε. 480

Ἔνθα μιν ἷκτο φέρουσα θοὴν διὰ νύκτα μέλαιναν

and stout Hades who dwells in halls under the earth, 455
who has a pitiless heart, and the loud-sounding earth-shaker
and all-wise Zeus, father of gods and men,
by whose thunder the wide earth trembles.
Them, great Kronos swallowed as each one came forth
from the divine womb to his mother's knees, 460
with this intent, that none of the noble sons of Ouranos
possesses royal honors amongst the immortals,
for he learned from Gaia and starry Ouranos
that he was destined to be overpowered by his own son,
although he himself was strong, through the cunning of the great Zeus. 465
Therefore, he had no blind outlook, but watching closely
swallowed his children, while Rhea suffered intensifying grief.
But when she was about to bear Zeus, the father of gods and men,
then she besought her own dear parents
Gaia and starry Ouranos, to form a plan with her 470
of how to have a secret birth of her lovely child,
retribution to the blood-guiltiness of the father
and the children who had been swallowed by great Kronos the wily.
And they, being persuaded, heard their dear daughter
and narrated all that was destined to happen 475
about Kronos the wily and his stout-hearted son.
So they sent her to Lyktos, to the rich land of Krete
when she was ready to bear the youngest of her children,
the great Zeus, whom gigantic earth did receive
in wide Krete to nurture and cherish. 480
Carrying him quickly in the dark night, she came first to Lyktos.

πρώτην ἐς Λύκτον· κρύψεν δέ ἑ χερσὶ λαβοῦσα

ἄντρῳ ἐν ἠλιβάτῳ, ζαθέης ὑπὸ κεύθεσι γαίης,

Αἰγαίῳ ἐν ὄρει πεπυκασμένῳ ὑλήεντι.

Τῷ δὲ σπαργανίσασα μέγαν λίθον ἐγγυάλιξεν   485

Οὐρανίδῃ μέγ᾽ ἄνακτι, θεῶν προτέρῳ βασιλῆι.

Τὸν τόθ᾽ ἑλὼν χείρεσσιν ἑὴν ἐσκάτθετο νηδὺν

σχέτλιος· οὐδ᾽ ἐνόησε μετὰ φρεσίν, ὥς οἱ ὀπίσσω

ἀντὶ λίθου ἑὸς υἱὸς ἀνίκητος καὶ ἀκηδὴς

λείπεθ᾽, ὅ μιν τάχ᾽ ἔμελλε βίῃ καὶ χερσὶ δαμάσσας   490

τιμῆς ἐξελάειν, ὃ δ᾽ ἐν ἀθανάτοισι ἀνάξειν.

Καρπαλίμως δ᾽ ἄρ᾽ ἔπειτα μένος καὶ φαίδιμα γυῖα

ηὔξετο τοῖο ἄνακτος· ἐπιπλομένων δ᾽ ἐνιαυτῶν

[Γαίης ἐννεσίῃσι πολυφραδέεσσι δολωθεὶς]

ὃν γόνον ἄψ ἀνέηκε μέγας Κρόνος ἀγκυλομήτης   495

νικηθεὶς τέχνῃσι βίηφί τε παιδὸς ἑοῖο.

Πρῶτον δ᾽ ἐξέμεσεν λίθον, πύματον καταπίνων·

τὸν μὲν Ζεὺς στήριξε κατὰ χθονὸς εὐρυοδείης

Πυθοῖ ἐν ἠγαθέῃ γυάλοις ὕπο Παρνησοῖο

σῆμ᾽ ἔμεν ἐξοπίσω, θαῦμα θνητοῖσι βροτοῖσιν.   500

[Λῦσε δὲ πατροκασιγνήτους ὀλοῶν ὑπὸ δεσμῶν

Οὐρανίδας, οὕς δῆσε πατὴρ ἀεσιφροσύνῃσιν·

οἵ οἱ ἀπεμνήσαντο χάριν εὐεργεσιάων,

δῶκαν δὲ βροντὴν ἠδ᾽ αἰθαλόεντα κεραυνὸν

καὶ στεροπήν· τὸ πρὶν δὲ πελώρη Γαῖα κεκεύθει·   505

τοῖς πίσυνος θνητοῖσι καὶ ἀθανάτοισιν ἀνάσσει.]

Κούρην δ᾽ Ἰαπετὸς καλλίσφυρον Ὠκεανίνην

ἠγάγετο Κλυμένην καὶ ὁμὸν λέχος εἰσανέβαινεν.

Gaia took him in her arms and hid him in a deep cave,

a crypt of the holy earth,

on the well-covered with wood Mount Aegaeon.

Rhea swathed a great stone and put it in the hands 485

of the great lord Kronos, king of the earlier gods.

Then he took it in his hands and thrust it in his stomach

unaware, not knowing in his heart that in place of the stone,

his son had been left behind, unconquered and pitiless,

who was destined soon to overpower Kronos by force and his hands 490

and remove his father's honors to reign over the immortal gods.

After that, the strength and the shining limbs of the master

were growing rapidly, and as the years passed by,

great Kronos the wily, being beguiled

by the wise suggestions of Gaia, he brought up again his children, 495

being conquered by the arts and force of his own son.

First, he disgorged the stone which he had swallowed last

and Zeus set that stone fast on the wide-pathed earth*

at very divine Pytho, under the dales of Parnassos,

to be a sign for hereafter and a marvel to mortal men. 500

And he set free from their fatal bonds the brothers of his father,

the sons of Ouranos (Ouranidai), whom their father in his foolishness had bound

and they didn't forget to be grateful to Zeus for his good offices

and they gave him thunder, the burning thunderbolt and lightning,

for before that, gigantic Gaia had them hidden. 505

In them, he trusts and rules over mortals and immortals.

Then Iapetos took the neat-ankled maid Klemene, daughter of Okeanos

and went up with her on to the marriage bed.

38 Metaphrasis: Dimitrios Kiriakopoulos

Ἡ δέ οἱ Ἄτλαντα κρατερόφρονα γείνατο παῖδα·
τίκτε δ' ὑπερκύδαντα Μενοίτιον ἠδὲ Προμηθέα, 510
ποικίλον αἰολόμητιν, ἁμαρτίνοόν τ' Ἐπιμηθέα,
ὅς κακὸν ἐξ ἀρχῆς γένετ' ἀνδράσιν ἀλφηστῇσιν·
πρῶτος γάρ ῥα Διὸς πλαστὴν ὑπέδεκτο γυναῖκα
παρθένον. Ὑβριστὴν δὲ Μενοίτιον εὐρύοπα Ζεὺς
εἰς Ἔρεβος κατέπεμψε βαλὼν ψολόεντι κεραυνῷ 515
εἵνεκ' ἀτασθαλίης τε καὶ ἠνορέης ὑπερόπλου.
Ἄτλας δ' οὐρανὸν εὐρὺν ἔχει κρατερῆς ὑπ' ἀνάγκης
πείρασιν ἐν γαίης, πρόπαρ Ἑσπερίδων λιγυφώνων,
ἑστηὼς κεφαλῇ τε καὶ ἀκαμάτῃσι χέρεσσιν·
ταύτην γάρ οἱ μοῖραν ἐδάσσατο μητίετα Ζεύς. 520
Δῆσε δ' ἀλυκτοπέδῃσι Προμηθέα ποικιλόβουλον
δεσμοῖς ἀργαλέοισι μέσον διὰ κίον' ἐλάσσας·
καί οἱ ἐπ' αἰετὸν ὦρσε τανύπτερον· αὐτὰρ ὅ γ' ἧπαρ
ἤσθιεν ἀθάνατον, τὸ δ' ἀέξετο ἶσον ἁπάντῃ
νυκτός, ὅσον πρόπαν ἦμαρ ἔδοι τανυσίπτερος ὄρνις. 525
Τὸν μὲν ἄρ' Ἀλκμήνης καλλισφύρου ἄλκιμος υἱὸς
Ἡρακλέης ἔκτεινε, κακὴν δ' ἀπὸ νοῦσον ἄλαλκεν
Ἰαπετιονίδῃ καὶ ἐλύσατο δυσφροσυνάων
οὐκ ἀέκητι Ζηνὸς Ὀλυμπίου ὑψιμέδοντος,
ὄφρ' Ἡρακλῆος Θηβαγενέος κλέος εἴη 530
πλεῖον ἔτ' ἢ τὸ πάροιθεν ἐπὶ χθόνα πουλυβότειραν.
Ταῦτά γ' ἄρ' ἀζόμενος τίμα ἀριδείκετον υἱόν·
καί περ χωόμενος παύθη χόλου, ὃν πρὶν ἔχεσκεν,
οὕνεκ' ἐρίζετο βουλὰς ὑπερμενέι Κρονίωνι.
Καὶ γὰρ ὅτ' ἐκρίνοντο θεοὶ θνητοί τ' ἄνθρωποι 535

Then she bore him a stout-hearted son, Atlas.
Also she bore super-glorious Menetios,
the versatile and full of various wiles Prometheus,
the erring in mind Epimetheus, who from the first was evil to laborious men,
for he was first submitted to a woman, the maid that Zeus had formed.
The wanton Menetios, Zeus the far-seeing, struck with smoky thunderbolt
and sent him down to Erebos
because of his arrogance and excessive bravery,
and Atlas, under hard constraint, upholds the wide sky
with unwearying head and arms, standing at the end of the earth
in front of the sweet-voiced Hesperidai.
This was his destiny assigned by the wise Zeus.
And the wily-minded Prometheus he bound with galling bonds
and painful chains, thrusted him to the middle of a pillar
and sent on him a long-winged eagle who fed on his immortal liver.
By night the liver enlarged as much
as the long-winged bird devoured all day long.
That bird Herakles slew, the strong son of beautiful-ankled Alkmene
and delivered the son of Iapetos from the cruel suffering,
not without the will of Olympian Zeus who reigns on high,
in order that the glory of Herakles, the Theban born,*
could be yet greater than it was before
on the all-nourishing earth. This he thought and honored
his most renowned son. He ceased from the wrath he had before,
being angry because Prometheus contended in counsels
against the almighty son of Kronos.
When the gods and mortal men came to issues in Mekone,

40   Metaphrasis: Dimitrios Kiriakopoulos

Μηκώνῃ, τότ' ἔπειτα μέγαν βοῦν πρόφρονι θυμῷ
δασσάμενος προέθηκε, Διὸς νόον ἐξαπαφίσκων.
Τοῖς μὲν γὰρ σάρκας τε καὶ ἔγκατα πίονα δημῷ
ἐν ῥινῷ κατέθηκε καλύψας γαστρὶ βοείῃ,
τῷ δ' αὖτ' ὀστέα λευκὰ βοὸς δολίῃ ἐπὶ τέχνῃ   540
εὐθετίσας κατέθηκε καλύψας ἀργέτι δημῷ.
Δὴ τότε μιν προσέειπε πατὴρ ἀνδρῶν τε θεῶν τε·
Ἰαπετιονίδη, πάντων ἀριδείκετ' ἀνάκτων,
ὦ πέπον, ὡς ἑτεροζήλως διεδάσσαο μοίρας.
Ὣς φάτο κερτομέων Ζεὺς ἄφθιτα μήδεα εἰδώς.   545
Τὸν δ' αὖτε προσέειπε Προμηθεὺς ἀγκυλομήτης
ἦκ' ἐπιμειδήσας, δολίης δ' οὐ λήθετο τέχνης·
Ζεῦ κύδιστε μέγιστε θεῶν αἰειγενετάων,
τῶν δ' ἕλε', ὁπποτέρην σε ἐνὶ φρεσὶ θυμὸς ἀνώγει.
Φῆ ῥα δολοφρονέων· Ζεὺς δ' ἄφθιτα μήδεα εἰδὼς   550
γνῶ ῥ' οὐδ' ἠγνοίησε δόλον· κακὰ δ' ὄσσετο θυμῷ
θνητοῖς ἀνθρώποισι, τὰ καὶ τελέεσθαι ἔμελλεν.
Χερσὶ δ' ὅ γ' ἀμφοτέρῃσιν ἀνείλετο λευκὸν ἄλειφαρ.
Χώσατο δὲ φρένας ἀμφί, χόλος δέ μιν ἵκετο θυμόν,
ὡς ἴδεν ὀστέα λευκὰ βοὸς δολίῃ ἐπὶ τέχνῃ.   555
Ἐκ τοῦ δ' ἀθανάτοισιν ἐπὶ χθονὶ φῦλ' ἀνθρώπων
καίουσ' ὀστέα λευκὰ θυηέντων ἐπὶ βωμῶν.
Τὸν δὲ μέγ' ὀχθήσας προσέφη νεφεληγερέτα Ζεύς·
Ἰαπετιονίδη, πάντων πέρι μήδεα εἰδώς,
ὦ πέπον, οὐκ ἄρα πω δολίης ἐπιλήθεο τέχνης.   560
Ὣς φάτο χωόμενος Ζεὺς ἄφθιτα μήδεα εἰδώς·
ἐκ τούτου δὴ ἔπειτα δόλου μεμνημένος αἰεὶ

Prometheus with forward mind cut up a great oxen

and set it before them, trying to deceive the mind of great Zeus.

For the rest, he did set the flesh and the inner fat parts upon the hide,

covering them with the oxen's paunch, but for Zeus,

he put the white bones of the ox, well arranged with deceitful art   540

and covered them with shining fat.

Then, the father of gods and men said to him,

"Son of Iapetos, most renowned of all lords,

my good friend, how unfairly you have divided the portions!"

In this way did Zeus speak, he whose wisdom is imperishable,   545

sneering at him, but wily Prometheus answered,

softly smiling and without forgetting his cunning wile,

"Zeus, most glorious and greatest of the eternal gods,

take whichever of these portions your heart desires."

So he said, thinking trickery, but Zeus, whose wisdom is imperishable,   550

was aware and was not deceived by the trick, and in his mind

he presaged evil against mortal men and was destined to execute.

With both hands, he lifted up the white fat;

he got angry in his mind and his heart got bitter

when he saw the white ox bones guilefuly crafted.   555

Since then, the tribes of men on earth

burn white bones to the immortals upon fragrant altars.

And cloud-compeller Zeus, being sorely angered, said to him,

"Son of Iapetos, the cleverest of all, my good friend,

you have not forgotten yet your cunning arts!"   560

So spoke Zeus in anger, who has imperishable wisdom.

After, because of that, he was mindful of the trick

42 Metaphrasis: Dimitrios Kiriakopoulos

οὐκ ἐδίδου μελίῃσι πυρὸς μένος ἀκαμάτοιο
θνητοῖς ἀνθρώποις, οἳ ἐπὶ χθονὶ ναιετάουσιν.
Ἀλλά μιν ἐξαπάτησεν ἐὺς πάις Ἰαπετοῖο   565
κλέψας ἀκαμάτοιο πυρὸς τηλέσκοπον αὐγὴν
ἐν κοΐλῳ νάρθηκι· δάκεν δέ ἑ νειόθι θυμόν,
Ζῆν᾽ ὑψιβρεμέτην, ἐχόλωσε δέ μιν φίλον ἦτορ,
ὡς ἴδ᾽ ἐν ἀνθρώποισι πυρὸς τηλέσκοπον αὐγήν.
Αὐτίκα δ᾽ ἀντὶ πυρὸς τεῦξεν κακὸν ἀνθρώποισιν·   570
γαίης γὰρ σύμπλασσε περικλυτὸς Ἀμφιγυήεις
παρθένῳ αἰδοίῃ ἴκελον Κρονίδεω διὰ βουλάς.
Ζῶσε δὲ καὶ κόσμησε θεὰ γλαυκῶπις Ἀθήνη
ἀργυφέῃ ἐσθῆτι· κατὰ κρῆθεν δὲ καλύπτρην
δαιδαλέην χείρεσσι κατέσχεθε, θαῦμα ἰδέσθαι·   575
[ἀμφὶ δέ οἱ στεφάνους, νεοθηλέος ἄνθεα ποίης,
ἱμερτοὺς περίθηκε καρήατι Παλλὰς Ἀθήνη.]
ἀμφὶ δέ οἱ στεφάνην χρυσέην κεφαλῆφιν ἔθηκε,
τὴν αὐτὸς ποίησε περικλυτὸς Ἀμφιγυήεις
ἀσκήσας παλάμῃσι, χαριζόμενος Διὶ πατρί.   580
Τῇ δ᾽ ἐνὶ δαίδαλα πολλὰ τετεύχατο, θαῦμα ἰδέσθαι,
κνώδαλ᾽, ὅσ᾽ ἤπειρος πολλὰ τρέφει ἠδὲ θάλασσα·
τῶν ὅ γε πόλλ᾽ ἐνέθηκε,—χάρις δ᾽ ἀπελάμπετο πολλή,—
θαυμάσια, ζῴοισιν ἐοικότα φωνήεσσιν.
Αὐτὰρ ἐπεὶ δὴ τεῦξε καλὸν κακὸν ἀντ᾽ ἀγαθοῖο,   585
ἐξάγαγ᾽, ἔνθα περ ἄλλοι ἔσαν θεοὶ ἠδ᾽ ἄνθρωποι,
κόσμῳ ἀγαλλομένην γλαυκώπιδος ὀβριμοπάτρης.
θαῦμα δ᾽ ἔχ᾽ ἀθανάτους τε θεοὺς θνητούς τ᾽ ἀνθρώπους,
ὡς εἶδον δόλον αἰπύν, ἀμήχανον ἀνθρώποισιν.

and he would not give to the Melian race of the mortal men
who dwell on earth the power of unwearying fire.
But the brave son of Iapetos beguiled him, 565
stealing the far-seen beam of unwearying fire,
in a hollow fennel stalk. The soul of high-thunderer Zeus
was deeply beaten and his dear heart got bitter
when he saw amongst men the far-seen beam.
At once he made ready an evil thing for men reprisals of the fire. 570
From earth the famous lame god (Hephestos) formed the likeness
of a shy maiden, to the wish of the son of Kronos.
And the goddess, bright-eyed Athena, girded and adorned by
silvery raiment, with her hands she spread down
from her head a broidered veil, a wonder to see. 575
And Pallas Athena put about her head lovely garlands,
flowers of new-grown grass. Also around her head
the famous lame god put a golden crown,
which he made himself with his own hands
as a favor to his father Zeus. 580
On it he made many curious designs, a wonder to see,
of the many beasts which the land and sea rears up,
too many wonderful things he put on it, like living beings with voices
and great beauty shone forth from it.
But when he had made the beautiful evil instead of good,* 585
he brought it out to the place where the other gods and men were.
She was delighted in the fashion, which the owl-eyed daughter
of the mighty one had given her. Wonder conquered the immortal gods
and mortal men, when they saw the perfect guile, invincible for men,

[ἐκ τῆς γὰρ γένος ἐστὶ γυναικῶν θηλυτεράων,]   590
τῆς γὰρ ὀλώιόν ἐστι γένος καὶ φῦλα γυναικῶν,
πῆμα μέγ᾽ αἵ θνητοῖσι μετ᾽ ἀνδράσι ναιετάουσιν
οὐλομένης πενίης οὐ σύμφοροι, ἀλλὰ κόροιο.
Ὡς δ᾽ ὁπότ᾽ ἐν σμήνεσσι κατηρεφέεσσι μέλισσαι
κηφῆνας βόσκωσι, κακῶν ξυνήονας ἔργων·   595
αἳ μέν τε πρόπαν ἦμαρ ἐς ἠέλιον καταδύντα
ἠμάτιαι σπεύδουσι τιθεῖσί τε κηρία λευκά,
οἳ δ᾽ ἔντοσθε μένοντες ἐπηρεφέας κατὰ σίμβλους
ἀλλότριον κάματον σφετέρην ἐς γαστέρ᾽ ἀμῶνται·
ὣς δ᾽ αὔτως ἄνδρεσσι κακὸν θνητοῖσι γυναῖκας   600
Ζεὺς ὑψιβρεμέτης θῆκεν, ξυνήονας ἔργων
ἀργαλέων· ἕτερον δὲ πόρεν κακὸν ἀντ᾽ ἀγαθοῖο·
ὅς κε γάμον φεύγων καὶ μέρμερα ἔργα γυναικῶν
μὴ γῆμαι ἐθέλῃ, ὀλοὸν δ᾽ ἐπὶ γῆρας ἵκοιτο
χήτεϊ γηροκόμοιο· ὅ γ᾽ οὐ βιότου ἐπιδευὴς   605
ζώει, ἀποφθιμένου δὲ διὰ κτῆσιν δατέονται
χηρωσταί· ᾧ δ᾽ αὖτε γάμου μετὰ μοῖρα γένηται,
κεδνὴν δ᾽ ἔσχεν ἄκοιτιν ἀρηρυῖαν πραπίδεσσι,
τῷ δέ τ᾽ ἀπ᾽ αἰῶνος κακὸν ἐσθλῷ ἀντιφερίζει
ἐμμενές· ὃς δέ κε τέτμῃ ἀταρτηροῖο γενέθλης,   610
ζώει ἐνὶ στήθεσσιν ἔχων ἀλίαστον ἀνίην
θυμῷ καὶ κραδίῃ, καὶ ἀνήκεστον κακόν ἐστιν.
Ὣς οὐκ ἔστι Διὸς κλέψαι νόον οὐδὲ παρελθεῖν.
Οὐδὲ γὰρ Ἰαπετιονίδης ἀκάκητα Προμηθεὺς
τοῖό γ᾽ ὑπεξήλυξε βαρὺν χόλον, ἀλλ᾽ ὑπ᾽ ἀνάγκης   615
καὶ πολύιδριν ἐόντα μέγας κατὰ δεσμὸς ἐρύκει.

as from her is the race of women, the female. 590

Of her is the fatal race and tribes of women, great misery,

who dwells with mortal men, not companion of the baneful poverty,

but only with wealth, and as in the vaulted hives bees feed the drones,

partners of bad works, while them, all day long until the sunset,

day by day, they eagerly make the white combs, 595

the drones stay in the covered beehives,

drawing into their belly the toil of others.

Similar evil for the mortal men laid high-thunderer Zeus,

women, partners of evil deeds.

And he gave them another evil instead of good. 600

Whoever avoids marriage and the baneful woman's works

and will not wed, reaches the deadly old age,

without anyone attending him.

Though he cannot live without his livelihood,

when he is dead, kinsfolk divide his possessions amongst them. 605

For the man again, who chooses the destiny of marriage

and has a careful wife with sound mind,

evil continually contends with good forever,

for, whoever has mischievous family

lives with unshrinking grief in his chest, in his mind, 610

and his heart, and this evil cannot be healed.

So, it is not possible the mind of Zeus to deceive, nor go beyond,

for not even the son of Iapetos, innocent Prometheus,

did escape his heavy anger, though he had much knowledge and wisdom,

but of necessity, strong bonds restrained him. 615

When first their father was vexed in his heart with Briareos,

46 Metaphrasis: Dimitrios Kiriakopoulos

Βριάρεῳ δ᾽ ὡς πρῶτα πατὴρ ὠδύσσατο θυμῷ

Κόττῳ τ᾽ ἠδὲ Γύῃ, δῆσεν κρατερῷ ἐνὶ δεσμῷ

ἠνορέην ὑπέροπλον ἀγώμενος ἠδὲ καὶ εἶδος

καὶ μέγεθος· κατένασσε δ᾽ ὑπὸ χθονὸς εὐρυοδείης.   620

Ἔνθ᾽ οἵ γ᾽ ἄλγε᾽ ἔχοντες ὑπὸ χθονὶ ναιετάοντες

ἧατ᾽ ἐπ᾽ ἐσχατιῇ, μεγάλης ἐν πείρασι γαίης,

δηθὰ μάλ᾽ ἀχνύμενοι, κραδίῃ μέγα πένθος ἔχοντες.

ἀλλά σφεας Κρονίδης τε καὶ ἀθάνατοι θεοὶ ἄλλοι,

οὓς τέκεν ἠύκομος Ῥείη Κρόνου ἐν φιλότητι,   625

Γαίης φραδμοσύνῃσιν ἀνήγαγον ἐς φάος αὖτις·

αὐτὴ γάρ σφιν ἅπαντα διηνεκέως κατέλεξε

σὺν κείνοις νίκην τε καὶ ἀγλαὸν εὖχος ἀρέσθαι.

δηρὸν γὰρ μάρναντο πόνον θυμαλγέ᾽ ἔχοντες

Τιτῆνές τε θεοὶ καὶ ὅσοι Κρόνου ἐξεγένοντο   630

ἀντίον ἀλλήλοισι διὰ κρατερὰς ὑσμίνας,

οἳ μὲν ἀφ᾽ ὑψηλῆς Ὄθρυος Τιτῆνες ἀγαυοί,

οἳ δ᾽ ἄρ᾽ ἀπ᾽ Οὐλύμποιο θεοί, δωτῆρες ἐάων,

οὓς τέκεν ἠύκομος Ῥείη Κρόνῳ εὐνηθεῖσα.

οἵ ῥα τότ᾽ ἀλλήλοισι χόλον θυμαλγέ᾽ ἔχοντες   635

συνεχέως ἐμάχοντο δέκα πλείους ἐνιαυτούς·

οὐδέ τις ἦν ἔριδος χαλεπῆς λύσις οὐδὲ τελευτὴ

οὐδετέροις, ἶσον δὲ τέλος τέτατο πτολέμοιο.

Ἀλλ᾽ ὅτε δὴ κείνοισι παρέσχεθεν ἄρμενα πάντα,

νέκταρ τ᾽ ἀμβροσίην τε, τά περ θεοὶ αὐτοὶ ἔδουσι,   640

πάντων ἐν στήθεσσιν ἀέξετο θυμὸς ἀγήνωρ.

[Ὡς νέκταρ τ᾽ ἐπάσαντο καὶ ἀμβροσίην ἐρατεινήν,]

δὴ τότε τοῖς μετέειπε πατὴρ ἀνδρῶν τε θεῶν τε·

Kottos, and Gyes, he bound them in cruel bonds, envying

their exceeding manhood, their shape, and great size.

He made them stay beneath the wide-pathed earth,

where they suffer living under the earth. 620

They sit at the end of the earth, at its great borders,

for long time distressed, having great sadness at heart.

But the son of Kronos and the other immortal gods,

whom beauty-haired Rhea bore, with the affection of Kronos,

brought them up again to the light, at Gaia's advising,* 625

for she herself distinctly recounted everything,

that with them, victory and glorious boast would gain

because the Titanes and as many as sprung from Kronos,

had long been fighting against each other

with heart-grieving toil in stubborn battles. 630

The noble Titanes (fighting) from high Othrys,

and the gods, givers of good,

whom beauty-haired Rhea bore

in union with Kronos, (fighting) from Olympos.

So they were fighting continuously for ten full years 635

with heart-grieving fight of one another, the hard strife

was not easing, there was no end for either side

and the war was evenly balanced.

But when the gods supplied them (the Hekatonkheires) with all the provisions,

nectar and ambrosia, which the gods themselves eat, 640

their proud spirit revived within them after they had fed

on nectar and fascinated ambrosia.

Then, the father of gods and men said to them,

κέκλυτε μευ, Γαίης τε καὶ Οὐρανοῦ ἀγλαὰ τέκνα,

ὄφρ᾽ εἴπω, τά με θυμὸς ἐνὶ στήθεσσι κελεύει. 645

Ἤδη γὰρ μάλα δηρὸν ἐναντίοι ἀλλήλοισι

νίκης καὶ κράτεος πέρι μαρνάμεθ᾽ ἤματα πάντα

Τιτῆνές τε θεοὶ καὶ ὅσοι Κρόνου ἐκγενόμεσθα.

Ὑμεῖς δὲ μεγάλην τε βίην καὶ χεῖρας ἀάπτους

φαίνετε Τιτήνεσσιν ἐναντίοι ἐν δαῖ λυγρῇ 650

μνησάμενοι φιλότητος ἐνηέος, ὅσσα παθόντες

ἐς φάος ἂψ ἀφίκεσθε δυσηλεγέος ὑπὸ δεσμοῦ

ἡμετέρας διὰ βουλὰς ὑπὸ ζόφου ἠερόεντος.

Ὣς φάτο· τὸν δ᾽ ἐξαῦτις ἀμείβετο Κόττος ἀμύμων·

δαιμόνι᾽, οὐκ ἀδάητα πιφαύσκεαι· ἀλλὰ καὶ αὐτοὶ 655

ἴδμεν, ὅ τοι περὶ μὲν πραπίδες, περὶ δ᾽ ἐστὶ νόημα,

ἀλκτὴρ δ᾽ ἀθανάτοισιν ἀρῆς γένεο κρυεροῖο.

Σῇσι δ᾽ ἐπιφροσύνῃσιν ὑπὸ ζόφου ἠερόεντος

ἄψορρον δεῦρ᾽ αὖτις ἀμειλίκτων ὑπὸ δεσμῶν

ἠλύθομεν, Κρόνου υἱὲ ἄναξ, ἀνάελπτα παθόντες. 660

Τῷ καὶ νῦν ἀτενεῖ τε νόῳ καὶ ἐπίφρονι βουλῇ

ῥυσόμεθα κράτος ὑμὸν ἐν αἰνῇ δηιοτῆτι

μαρνάμενοι Τιτῆσιν ἀνὰ κρατερὰς ὑσμίνας.

Ὣς φάτ᾽· ἐπήνεσσαν δὲ θεοί, δωτῆρες ἑάων,

μῦθον ἀκούσαντες· πολέμου δ᾽ ἐλιλαίετο θυμὸς 665

μᾶλλον ἔτ᾽ ἢ τὸ πάροιθε· μάχην δ᾽ ἀμέγαρτον ἔγειραν

πάντες, θήλειαί τε καὶ ἄρσενες, ἤματι κείνῳ,

Τιτῆνές τε θεοὶ καὶ ὅσοι Κρόνου ἐξεγένοντο,

οὕς τε Ζεὺς Ἐρέβεσφιν ὑπὸ χθονὸς ἧκε φόωσδε

δεινοί τε κρατεροί τε, βίην ὑπέροπλον ἔχοντες. 670

"Hear me, splendid children of Gaia and Ouranos.
I may say what the heart in my chest bids.
Already, for too long, we are facing in fight,
every day struggling for victory and dominance,
the Titan gods and as many as we sprung from Kronos.
But, you have to show your great power and your invincible arms
against the Titanes, in ruinous battle.
Remember our friendly kindness and what you suffer,
before you come back to the light, from your deadly bonds
and the misty gloom, through our counsels."
So he said. And noble Kottos replied,
"Divine one, you are not telling us unknown things.
We know ourselves that your mind and understanding is exceeding
and you defend the immortals from the chilling curse
and through your thoughtfulness we came back again
from the misty gloom and the cruel bonds,
enjoying the unexpected, oh Lord, son of Kronos,
so now, with strained mind and zealous heart,
we will save your power in dreadful strife
and fight the Titanes in hard battles."
So he said, and the gods, givers of good things,
applauded when they heard his speech. Their soul had desire for war
even more than before and they all, both male and female,
stirred up a terrible battle that day,
the Titan gods and all who were born of Kronos,
with the ones Zeus brought to light from Erebos, beneath the earth,
the terrible and mighty who had excessive force.

Τῶν ἑκατὸν μὲν χεῖρες ἀπ' ὤμων ἀίσσοντο
πᾶσιν ὁμῶς, κεφαλαὶ δὲ ἑκάστῳ πεντήκοντα
ἐξ ὤμων ἐπέφυκον ἐπὶ στιβαροῖσι μέλεσσιν.
Οἳ τότε Τιτήνεσσι κατέσταθεν ἐν δαῖ λυγρῇ
πέτρας ἠλιβάτους στιβαρῆς ἐν χερσὶν ἔχοντες. 675
Τιτῆνες δ' ἑτέρωθεν ἐκαρτύναντο φάλαγγας
προφρονέως, χειρῶν τε βίης θ' ἅμα ἔργον ἔφαινον
ἀμφότεροι· δεινὸν δὲ περίαχε πόντος ἀπείρων,
γῆ δὲ μέγ' ἐσμαράγησεν, ἐπέστενε δ' οὐρανὸς εὐρὺς
σειόμενος, πεδόθεν δὲ τινάσσετο μακρὸς Ὄλυμπος 680
ῥιπῇ ὕπ' ἀθανάτων, ἔνοσις δ' ἵκανε βαρεῖα
Τάρταρον ἠερόεντα, ποδῶν τ' αἰπεῖα ἰωὴ
ἀσπέτου ἰωχμοῖο βολάων τε κρατεράων·
Ὣς ἄρ' ἐπ' ἀλλήλοις ἵεσαν βέλεα στονόεντα.
Φωνὴ δ' ἀμφοτέρων ἵκετ' οὐρανὸν ἀστερόεντα 685
κεκλομένων· οἳ δὲ ξύνισαν μεγάλῳ ἀλαλητῷ.
Οὐδ' ἄρ' ἔτι Ζεὺς ἴσχεν ἑὸν μένος, ἀλλά νυ τοῦ γε
εἴθαρ μὲν μένεος πλῆντο φρένες, ἐκ δέ τε πᾶσαν
φαῖνε βίην· ἄμυδις δ' ἄρ' ἀπ' οὐρανοῦ ἠδ' ἀπ' Ὀλύμπου
ἀστράπτων ἔστειχε συνωχαδόν· οἱ δὲ κεραυνοὶ 690
ἴκταρ ἅμα βροντῇ τε καὶ ἀστεροπῇ ποτέοντο
χειρὸς ἄπο στιβαρῆς, ἱερὴν φλόγα εἰλυφόωντες
ταρφέες· ἀμφὶ δὲ γαῖα φερέσβιος ἐσμαράγιζε
καιομένη, λάκε δ' ἀμφὶ πυρὶ μεγάλ' ἄσπετος ὕλη.
Ἔζεε δὲ χθὼν πᾶσα καὶ Ὠκεανοῖο ῥέεθρα 695
πόντος τ' ἀτρύγετος· τοὺς δ' ἄμφεπε θερμὸς ἀυτμὴ
Τιτῆνας χθονίους, φλὸξ δ' αἰθέρα δῖαν ἵκανεν

From their shoulders, one hundred hands were quickly moving,

all alike, and each one had fifty heads

growing from the shoulders, upon stout limbs.

Then, they stood against the Titanes, in a baneful battle,*

holding enormous rocks in their strong hands.   675

On the other side, the Titanes strengthened their ranks

and eagerly both sides at the same time

showed the work of their hands and their might.

The boundless sea echoed terribly and the earth crashed loudly,

the wide sky groaned, shaking, and high Olympos was quaking from its foundation,   680

from the throwing of the immortal gods, and the heavy quaking

reached hazy Tartaros, just as the loud sound of their feet

and the unspeakable clatter of their hard missiles were heard.

This way they were launching one another mournful bolts, while the war-cry

of both sides was reaching the starry sky as they were shouting and they collided   685

with a great battle-cry. Nor yet Zeus was holding back his force

but at once his heart was filled with fury

and he showed forth all his strength.

Simultaneously, from the sky and from Olympos,

lightning bolts were repeatedly launched. The thunderbolts flew thick   690

from his strong hand, followed closely by thunder and lightning's

whirling hallow flame.

The life-giving earth clattered and burned all around

and the unspeakably vast wood crackled loudly with fire throughout

all the land. The ocean's streams and the unfruitful sea were boiling.   695

The hot breath enveloped the earth-born Titans.

The unspeakable flame was reaching the divine aether.

ἄσπετος, ὄσσε δ' ἄμερδε καὶ ἰφθίμων περ ἐόντων

αὐγὴ μαρμαίρουσα κεραυνοῦ τε στεροπῆς τε.

Καῦμα δὲ θεσπέσιον κάτεχεν Χάος· εἴσατο δ' ἄντα 700

ὀφθαλμοῖσιν ἰδεῖν ἠδ' οὔασι ὄσσαν ἀκοῦσαι

αὔτως, ὡς εἰ Γαῖα καὶ Οὐρανὸς εὐρὺς ὕπερθε

πίλνατο· τοῖος γάρ κε μέγας ὑπὸ δοῦπος ὀρώρει

τῆς μὲν ἐρειπομένης, τοῦ δ' ὑψόθεν ἐξεριπόντος·

τόσσος δοῦπος ἔγεντο θεῶν ἔριδι ξυνιόντων. 705

Σὺν δ' ἄνεμοι ἔνοσίν τε κονίην τ' ἐσφαράγιζον

βροντήν τε στεροπήν τε καὶ αἰθαλόεντα κεραυνόν,

κῆλα Διὸς μεγάλοιο, φέρον δ' ἰαχήν τ' ἐνοπήν τε

ἐς μέσον ἀμφοτέρων· ὄτοβος δ' ἄπλητος ὀρώρει

σμερδαλέης ἔριδος, κάρτος δ' ἀνεφαίνετο ἔργων. 710

Ἐκλίνθη δὲ μάχη· πρὶν δ' ἀλλήλοις ἐπέχοντες

ἐμμενέως ἐμάχοντο διὰ κρατερὰς ὑσμίνας.

Οἳ δ' ἄρ' ἐνὶ πρώτοισι μάχην δριμεῖαν ἔγειραν

Κόττος τε Βριάρεώς τε Γύης τ' ἄατος πολέμοιο,

οἵ ῥα τριηκοσίας πέτρας στιβαρῶν ἀπὸ χειρῶν 715

πέμπον ἐπασσυτέρας, κατὰ δ' ἐσκίασαν βελέεσσι

Τιτῆνας, καὶ τοὺς μὲν ὑπὸ χθονὸς εὐρυοδείης

πέμψαν καὶ δεσμοῖσιν ἐν ἀργαλέοισιν ἔδησαν

χερσὶν νικήσαντες ὑπερθύμους περ ἐόντας,

τόσσον ἔνερθ' ὑπὸ γῆς, ὅσον οὐρανός ἐστ' ἀπὸ γαίης· 720

[τόσσον γάρ τ' ἀπὸ γῆς ἐς Τάρταρον ἠερόεντα.]

Ἐννέα γὰρ νύκτας τε καὶ ἤματα χάλκεος ἄκμων

οὐρανόθεν κατιὼν δεκάτῃ κ' ἐς γαῖαν ἵκοιτο·

ἐννέα δ' αὖ νύκτας τε καὶ ἤματα χάλκεος ἄκμων

The flashing glare of the thunderbolt and lightning

blinded their eyes, though they were vigorous.

Khaos was seized fast by divine heat. 700

The sight for the eyes and the sound for the ears

seemed as if earth and the wide sky above came together,

for such a mighty sound would have risen as if earth were falling in ruins,

and the sky from high above was collapsing. So, loud sound was produced

from the gods while they were meeting in battle. 705

Also, the winds were bursting with quakes, dust, thunder,

lightning, and burning thunderbolts,

which are the arrows of great Zeus,

carrying loud noise and war-cry on both sides.

A horrible din of hideous strife arose and mighty deeds were shown. 710

The tide of war was turned, but until then they kept at one another

and, unceasing, were fighting in cruel battles.

Among the foremost who raised fierce combat

were Kottos and Briareos and Gyes, insatiable for war.

Three hundred rocks, one after another, they were discharging 715

from their strong hands and they overshadowed the Titanes

with their throws and they sent them beneath the wide-pathed earth

and bound them in painful fetters

when they had overpowered them with their hands,

though they were high-spirited. 720

So below under the earth they sent them as much as the sky

abstains from earth; so much from the earth to murky Tartaros.

For a brazen anvil falling down from sky,• for nine nights and days

would reach the earth upon the tenth, and again, a brazen anvil

ἐκ γαίης κατιὼν δεκάτῃ κ' ἐς Τάρταρον ἵκοι. 725
Τὸν πέρι χάλκεον ἕρκος ἐλήλαται· ἀμφὶ δέ μιν νὺξ
τριστοιχεὶ κέχυται περὶ δειρήν· αὐτὰρ ὕπερθεν
γῆς ῥίζαι πεφύασι καὶ ἀτρυγέτοιο θαλάσσης.
Ἔνθα θεοὶ Τιτῆνες ὑπὸ ζόφῳ ἠερόεντι
κεκρύφαται βουλῇσι Διὸς νεφεληγερέταο 730
[χώρῳ ἐν εὐρώεντι, πελώρης ἔσχατα γαίης.]
Τοῖς οὐκ ἐξιτόν ἐστι. θύρας δ' ἐπέθηκε Ποσειδέων
χαλκείας, τεῖχος δὲ περοίχεται ἀμφοτέρωθεν.
Ἔνθα Γύης Κόττος τε καὶ Ὀβριάρεως μεγάθυμος
ναίουσιν, φύλακες πιστοὶ Διὸς αἰγιόχοιο. 735
Ἔνθα δὲ γῆς δνοφερῆς καὶ Ταρτάρου ἠερόεντος
πόντου τ' ἀτρυγέτοιο καὶ οὐρανοῦ ἀστερόεντος
ἑξείης πάντων πηγαὶ καὶ πείρατ' ἔασιν
ἀργαλέ' εὐρώεντα, τά τε στυγέουσι θεοί περ,
χάσμα μέγ', οὐδέ κε πάντα τελεσφόρον εἰς ἐνιαυτὸν 740
οὖδας ἵκοιτ', εἰ πρῶτα πυλέων ἔντοσθε γένοιτο.
[Ἀλλά κεν ἔνθα καὶ ἔνθα φέροι πρὸ θύελλα θυέλλῃ
ἀργαλέη· δεινὸν δὲ καὶ ἀθανάτοισι θεοῖσι
τοῦτο τέρας. Νυκτὸς δ' ἐρεβεννῆς οἰκία δεινὰ
ἕστηκεν νεφέλης κεκαλυμμένα κυανέῃσιν.] 745
Τῶν πρόσθ' Ἰαπετοῖο πάις ἔχει οὐρανὸν εὐρὺν
ἑστηὼς κεφαλῇ τε καὶ ἀκαμάτῃσι χέρεσσιν
ἀστεμφέως, ὅθι Νύξ τε καὶ Ἡμέρη ἆσσον ἰοῦσαι
ἀλλήλας προσέειπον, ἀμειβόμεναι μέγαν οὐδὸν
χάλκεον· ἣ μὲν ἔσω καταβήσεται, ἣ δὲ θύραζε 750
ἔρχεται, οὐδέ ποτ' ἀμφοτέρας δόμος ἐντὸς ἐέργει,

falling from earth for nine nights and days would reach Tartaros upon the tenth.   725
Bronze fence invests him and three rows of night
is poured around his neck, while above grow the roots of the earth
and unfruitful sea. There, by the counsel of cloud-compeller Zeus,
the Titan gods are covered in the earth,
under misty gloom,   730
in a dark place, at the end of the giant earth,
for whom there is no coming out. Poseidon laid out
bronze gates and a wall runs all around it, on every side.
There, Gyes, Kottos, and high-minded Briareos dwell,
trusty warders of aegiokhos Zeus.   735
And there, all in their order, are the sources
and ends of the gloomy earth and misty Tartaros
and the unfruitful sea and starry sky,
painful and dark, which even the gods hate.
The great chasm, that if you pass the gate,   740
you never reach the bottom in a year's time,
but bears you here and there furious blast after blast
and this marvel is awful, even to the immortal gods.
There stands the fearful home of gloomy night,
wrapped in dark clouds.   745
In front of them, the son of Iapetos, unmoved,
holds the wide sky upon his head and untiring hands.
Where night and day meet and greet one another
as they pass the great bronze gate, and while the one is going down,
the other comes out of the door   750
and the house never holds them both within,

56   Metaphrasis: Dimitrios Kiriakopoulos

ἀλλ᾽ αἰεὶ ἑτέρη γε δόμων ἔκτοσθεν ἐοῦσα
γαῖαν ἐπιστρέφεται, ἣ δ᾽ αὖ δόμου ἐντὸς ἐοῦσα
μίμνει τὴν αὐτῆς ὥρην ὁδοῦ, ἔστ᾽ ἂν ἵκηται,
ἣ μὲν ἐπιχθονίοισι φάος πολυδερκὲς ἔχουσα,   755
ἣ δ᾽ Ὕπνον μετὰ χερσί, κασίγνητον Θανάτοιο.
Νὺξ ὀλοή, νεφέλῃ κεκαλυμμένη ἠεροειδεῖ.
Ἔνθα δὲ Νυκτὸς παῖδες ἐρεμνῆς οἰκί᾽ ἔχουσιν,
Ὕπνος καὶ Θάνατος, δεινοὶ θεοί· οὐδέ ποτ᾽ αὐτοὺς
Ἠέλιος φαέθων ἐπιδέρκεται ἀκτίνεσσιν   760
οὐρανὸν εἰς ἀνιὼν οὐδ᾽ οὐρανόθεν καταβαίνων.
Τῶν δ᾽ ἕτερος γαῖάν τε καὶ εὐρέα νῶτα θαλάσσης
ἥσυχος ἀνστρέφεται καὶ μείλιχος ἀνθρώποισι,
τοῦ δὲ σιδηρέη μὲν κραδίη, χάλκεον δέ οἱ ἦτορ
νηλεὲς ἐν στήθεσσιν· ἔχει δ᾽ ὃν πρῶτα λάβῃσιν   765
ἀνθρώπων· ἐχθρὸς δὲ καὶ ἀθανάτοισι θεοῖσιν.
Ἔνθα θεοῦ χθονίου πρόσθεν δόμοι ἠχήεντες
[ἰφθίμου τ᾽ Ἀίδεω καὶ ἐπαινῆς Περσεφονείης]
ἑστᾶσιν, δεινὸς δὲ κύων προπάροιθε φυλάσσει
νηλειής, τέχνην δὲ κακὴν ἔχει· ἐς μὲν ἰόντας   770
σαίνει ὁμῶς οὐρῇ τε καὶ οὔασιν ἀμφοτέροισιν,
ἐξελθεῖν δ᾽ οὐκ αὖτις ἐᾷ πάλιν, ἀλλὰ δοκεύων
ἐσθίει, ὅν κε λάβῃσι πυλέων ἔκτοσθεν ἰόντα.
[ἰφθίμου τ᾽ Ἀίδεω καὶ ἐπαινῆς Περσεφονείης.]
Ἔνθα δὲ ναιετάει στυγερὴ θεὸς ἀθανάτοισι,   775
δεινὴ Στύξ, θυγάτηρ ἀψορρόου Ὠκεανοῖο
πρεσβυτάτη· νόσφιν δὲ θεῶν κλυτὰ δώματα ναίει
μακρῇσιν πέτρῃσι κατηρεφέ᾽· ἀμφὶ δὲ πάντῃ

but always, one is outside the house passing over the earth
while the other stays at home
waiting for the time of her journey to come.
The one having much-seeing light for men on earth, 755
but the other holds in her hands Sleep, the brother of Death.
The deadly night, wrapped in dark cloud.
There, the children of swarthy night have their dwellings,
Sleep and Death, dreadful gods. The shining sun
never looks upon them with his beams, 760
not as he goes up in the sky, nor as from the sky comes down.
The one of them roams peacefully over the earth and
the sea's wide surface and is gentle to humans, but the other
has a heart of steel, a bronze and pitiless soul in his chest,
and he holds fast at once whomsoever of men he seizes 765
and he is an enemy also of the immortal gods.
There, in front, stand the clamorous chambers of the god
of the underworld, stout Hades and dreadful Persephone,
a fearful and pitiless dog is guarding the house in front
and he has a wicked method. To those who are coming in, 770
he wags his tail and both his ears, but he would not
let them go back out, and watching closely,
he devours whomsoever he catches going out of the gates
of stout Hades and dreadful Persephone.
And there dwells the goddess who is hated by the immortals, 775
the terrible Styx, eldest daughter of the refluent Okeanos.
Apart from the gods, in splendid halls she dwells,
vaulted over with long shelves of stone

58   Metaphrasis: Dimitrios Kiriakopoulos

κίοσιν ἀργυρέοισι πρὸς οὐρανὸν ἐστήρικται.
Παῦρα δὲ Θαύμαντος θυγάτηρ πόδας ὠκέα Ἶρις   780
ἀγγελίην πωλεῖται ἐπ᾽ εὐρέα νῶτα θαλάσσης.
Ὁππότ᾽ ἔρις καὶ νεῖκος ἐν ἀθανάτοισιν ὄρηται
καί ῥ᾽ ὅς τις ψεύδηται Ὀλύμπια δώματ᾽ ἐχόντων,
Ζεὺς δέ τε Ἶριν ἔπεμψε θεῶν μέγαν ὅρκον ἐνεῖκαι
τηλόθεν ἐν χρυσέῃ προχόῳ πολυώνυμον ὕδωρ   785
ψυχρόν, ὅτ᾽ ἐκ πέτρης καταλείβεται ἠλιβάτοιο
ὑψηλῆς· πολλὸν δὲ ὑπὸ χθονὸς εὐρυοδείης
ἐξ ἱεροῦ ποταμοῖο ῥέει διὰ νύκτα μέλαιναν
Ὠκεανοῖο κέρας· δεκάτη δ᾽ ἐπὶ μοῖρα δέδασται·
ἐννέα μὲν περὶ γῆν τε καὶ εὐρέα νῶτα θαλάσσης   790
δίνῃς ἀργυρέῃς εἰλιγμένος εἰς ἅλα πίπτει,
ἡ δὲ μί᾽ ἐκ πέτρης προρέει μέγα πῆμα θεοῖσιν.
Ὅς κεν τὴν ἐπίορκον ἀπολλείψας ἐπομόσσῃ
ἀθανάτων, οἳ ἔχουσι κάρη νιφόεντος Ὀλύμπου,
κεῖται νήυτμος τετελεσμένον εἰς ἐνιαυτόν·   795
οὐδέ ποτ᾽ ἀμβροσίης καὶ νέκταρος ἔρχεται ἆσσον
βρώσιος, ἀλλά τε κεῖται ἀνάπνευστος καὶ ἄναυδος
στρωτοῖς ἐν λεχέεσσι, κακὸν δέ ἑ κῶμα καλύπτει.
Αὐτὰρ ἐπεὶ νοῦσον τελέσῃ μέγαν εἰς ἐνιαυτόν,
ἄλλος γ᾽ ἐξ ἄλλου δέχεται χαλεπώτερος ἄεθλος.   800
Εἰνάετες δὲ θεῶν ἀπαμείρεται αἰὲν ἐόντων,
οὐδέ ποτ᾽ ἐς βουλὴν ἐπιμίσγεται οὐδ᾽ ἐπὶ δαῖτας
ἐννέα πάντα ἔτεα· δεκάτῳ δ᾽ ἐπιμίσγεται αὖτις
εἴρας ἐς ἀθανάτων, οἳ Ὀλύμπια δώματ᾽ ἔχουσιν.
Τοῖον ἄρ᾽ ὅρκον ἔθεντο θεοὶ Στυγὸς ἄφθιτον ὕδωρ   805

and propped up to the sky all around with silver pillars.
The daughter of Thaumas, swift-footed Iris, 780
rarely brings to her a message over the sea's wide surface.
Whenever strife and quarrel bursts out between the immortals,
and when any of them who lives in the Olympian halls lies,
then Zeus sends Iris to bring in golden jug
the great oath of the gods from far away. The famous cold water 785
which drops down from a high and steep rock,
a branch of the ocean, which flows through the dark night
out of the holy river, far under the wide-pathed earth.
The one-tenth was given to her; the other nine are swirling
around the earth and the sea's wide surface 790
in silver whirling and winding up, they fall into the sea.
The tenth flows out from a rock, big suffering for the gods,
for whoever of the immortals that hold the summit of snowy Olympos
pours a libation and takes an oath swearing falsely,
lays breathless until a full year is completed 795
and never comes near to taste ambrosia and nectar,
but lays breathless and silent on the bedspreads
and a deep trance covers him.
But when he completes a year, in his vast sickness,
another harder task follows after the first. 800
For nine years he is deprived of the eternal gods
and never joins their counsels and their feasts—
nine full years. But in the tenth year, he joins again the assemblies
of the immortal gods who hold the Olympian homes.
Such an oath, then, did the gods appoint, the eternal and primaeval 805

ώγύγιον, τὸ δ' ἵησι καταστυφέλου διὰ χώρου.

[Ἔνθα δὲ γῆς δνοφερῆς καὶ Ταρτάρου ἠερόεντος
πόντου τ' ἀτρυγέτοιο καὶ οὐρανοῦ ἀστερόεντος
ἑξείης πάντων πηγαὶ καὶ πείρατ' ἔασιν
ἀργαλέ' εὐρώεντα, τά τε στυγέουσι θεοί περ. 810
Ἔνθα δὲ μαρμάρεαί τε πύλαι καὶ χάλκεος οὐδὸς
ἀστεμφής, ῥίζῃσι διηνεκέεσσιν ἀρηρώς,
αὐτοφυής· πρόσθεν δὲ θεῶν ἔκτοσθεν ἀπάντων
Τιτῆνες ναίουσι, πέρην Χάεος ζοφεροῖο.
Αὐτὰρ ἐρισμαράγοιο Διὸς κλειτοὶ ἐπίκουροι 815
δώματα ναιετάουσιν ἐπ' Ὠκεανοῖο θεμέθλοις,
Κόττος τ' ἠδὲ Γύης· Βριάρεών γε μὲν ἠὺν ἐόντα
γαμβρὸν ἑὸν ποίησε βαρύκτυπος Ἐννοσίγαιος,
δῶκε δὲ Κυμοπόλειαν ὀπυίειν, θυγατέρα ἥν.]
Αὐτὰρ ἐπεὶ Τιτῆνας ἀπ' οὐρανοῦ ἐξέλασεν Ζεύς, 820
ὁπλότατον τέκε παῖδα Τυφωέα Γαῖα πελώρη
Ταρτάρου ἐν φιλότητι διὰ χρυσέην Ἀφροδίτην·
οὗ χεῖρες μὲν ἔασιν ἐπ' ἰσχύι, ἔργματ' ἔχουσαι,
καὶ πόδες ἀκάματοι κρατεροῦ θεοῦ· ἐκ δέ οἱ ὤμων
ἦν ἑκατὸν κεφαλαὶ ὄφιος, δεινοῖο δράκοντος, 825
γλώσσῃσιν δνοφερῇσι λελιχμότες, ἐκ δέ οἱ ὄσσων
θεσπεσίῃς κεφαλῇσιν ὑπ' ὀφρύσι πῦρ ἀμάρυσσεν
[πασέων δ' ἐκ κεφαλέων πῦρ καίετο δερκομένοιο]
φωναὶ δ' ἐν πάσῃσιν ἔσαν δεινῇς κεφαλῇσι
παντοίην ὄπ' ἰεῖσαι ἀθέσφατον· ἄλλοτε μὲν γὰρ 830
φθέγγονθ' ὥστε θεοῖσι συνιέμεν, ἄλλοτε δ' αὖτε
ταύρου ἐριβρύχεω, μένος ἀσχέτου, ὄσσαν ἀγαύρου,

water of Styx to be, and it flows through a rugged place.
And there, all in order are the sources and ends
of the dark earth, misty Tartaros
and the unfruitful sea and starry sky,
painful and moldy, which even the gods abhor.　　　　　　　　　　810
And there are the gleaming gates and the immovable
bronze threshold, joined together with unending roots,
self grown. And in front, away from all the gods,
live the Titanes, beyond gloomy Khaos.
But the glorious allies of loud-thundering Zeus,　　　　　　　　　　815
Kottos and Gyes, dwell in homes which have their foundations
upon the bottom of the ocean, yet brave Briareos,
the heavy-sounding earth-shaker, made his son-in-law
when he gave him Kymopolea, his daughter, to wed.
But when Zeus had driven out the Titanes from the sky,　　　　　　　820
giant Gaia bore her youngest child, Typhoeus,
of the affection of Tartaros, and by the aid of golden Aphrodite.
The hands of the powerful god were for vigorous deeds
and the legs were untiring. From his shoulders grew
one hundred heads of a snake, a fearful dragon,　　　　　　　　　　825
playing with their flickering black tongues. And under the brows of the eyes
of his awful heads, embers were sparkling.
Fire was burning from all his heads as he glared.
Voices emanated from all the dreadful heads,
uttering every kind of unspeakable sound. At one time,　　　　　　　830
they sounded as if they were understood to the gods, but at another,
the noise of a loud-bellowing bull resounded with proud and ungovernable fury,

62   Metaphrasis: Dimitrios Kiriakopoulos

ἄλλοτε δ᾽ αὖτε λέοντος ἀναιδέα θυμὸν ἔχοντος,

ἄλλοτε δ᾽ αὖ σκυλάκεσσιν ἐοικότα, θαύματ᾽ ἀκοῦσαι,

ἄλλοτε δ᾽ αὖ ῥοίζεσχ᾽, ὑπὸ δ᾽ ἤχεεν οὔρεα μακρά.   835

Καί νύ κεν ἔπλετο ἔργον ἀμήχανον ἤματι κείνῳ

καί κεν ὅ γε θνητοῖσι καὶ ἀθανάτοισιν ἄναξεν,

εἰ μὴ ἄρ᾽ ὀξὺ νόησε πατὴρ ἀνδρῶν τε θεῶν τε.

Σκληρὸν δ᾽ ἐβρόντησε καὶ ὄβριμον, ἀμφὶ δὲ γαῖα

σμερδαλέον κονάβησε καὶ οὐρανὸς εὐρὺς ὕπερθε   840

πόντος τ᾽ Ὠκεανοῦ τε ῥοαὶ καὶ Τάρταρα γαίης.

Ποσσὶ δ᾽ ὕπ᾽ ἀθανάτοισι μέγας πελεμίζετ᾽ Ὄλυμπος

ὀρνυμένοιο ἄνακτος· ἐπεστενάχιζε δὲ γαῖα.

Καῦμα δ᾽ ὑπ᾽ ἀμφοτέρων κάτεχεν ἰοειδέα πόντον

βροντῆς τε στεροπῆς τε, πυρός τ᾽ ἀπὸ τοῖο πελώρου,   845

[πρηστήρων ἀνέμων τε κεραυνοῦ τε φλεγέθοντος.]

ἔζεε δὲ χθὼν πᾶσα καὶ οὐρανὸς ἠδὲ θάλασσα

θυῖε δ᾽ ἄρ᾽ ἀμφ᾽ ἀκτὰς περί τ᾽ ἀμφί τε κύματα μακρὰ

ῥιπῇ ὕπ᾽ ἀθανάτων, ἔνοσις δ᾽ ἄσβεστος ὀρώρει

τρέε δ᾽ Ἀίδης, ἐνέροισι καταφθιμένοισιν ἀνάσσων,   850

Τιτῆνές θ᾽ ὑποταρτάριοι, Κρόνον ἀμφὶς ἐόντες,

[ἀσβέστου κελάδοιο καὶ αἰνῆς δηιοτῆτος.]

Ζεὺς δ᾽ ἐπεὶ οὖν κόρθυνεν ἑὸν μένος, εἵλετο δ᾽ ὅπλα,

βροντήν τε στεροπήν τε καὶ αἰθαλόεντα κεραυνόν,

πλῆξεν ἀπ᾽ Οὐλύμποιο ἐπάλμενος· ἀμφὶ δὲ πάσας   855

ἔπρεσε θεσπεσίας κεφαλὰς δεινοῖο πελώρου.

Αὐτὰρ ἐπεὶ δή μιν δάμασεν πληγῇσιν ἱμάσσας,

ἤριπε γυιωθείς, στενάχιζε δὲ γαῖα πελώρη.

Φλὸξ δὲ κεραυνωθέντος ἀπέσσυτο τοῖο ἄνακτος

and at another, the sound of a lion relentless in heart, but at another,

sounds like puppies, wonderful to hear, and again, at another moment,

he would hiss so that the lofty mountains would resound. 835

And that day would have happened an irreparable matter

and he would have come to rule over mortals and immortals,

if at once the father of gods and men had not perceived it.

Zeus thundered hard and mightily, and the earth around

and the wide sky above and the sea and the ocean currents 840

and the nether parts of the earth resounded terribly.

Great Olympos was trembling beneath the divine feet of the king

as he arose. The earth was groaning.

Between Zeus and Typhoeus, burning heat was taking hold of the dark blue sea

through the thunder and lightning, and through the fire of the monster 845

and the scorching winds of the burning thunderbolt.

All the earth, the sky, and the sea was boiling.

Long waves raged around the headlands

from the force of the immortals and an endless earthquake arose.

Hades was trembling (where he rules over the dead below 850

and the Titans who live under Tartaros with Kronos)

from the unending clamor and the cruel battle.

So when Zeus stimulated his own ire, seized his heavy arms,

thunder and lightning and burning thunderbolt

and assailant from Olympos struck the terrible monster 855

and burned all around his dreadful heads.

Since Zeus had conquered by smiting him with strokes

and Typhoeus was hurled down lame, the giant earth was groaning.

The flame of the thunderbolt-stricken lord

οὔρεος ἐν βήσσησιν Αἴτνης παιπαλοέσσης, 860
πληγέντος. Πολλὴ δὲ πελώρη καίετο γαῖα
ἀτμῇ θεσπεσίῃ καὶ ἐτήκετο κασσίτερος ὣς
τέχνῃ ὕπ' αἰζηῶν ἐν ἐυτρήτοις χοάνοισι
θαλφθείς, ἠὲ σίδηρος, ὅ περ κρατερώτατός ἐστιν,
οὔρεος ἐν βήσσησι δαμαζόμενος πυρὶ κηλέῳ 865
τήκεται ἐν χθονὶ δίῃ ὑφ' Ἡφαίστου παλάμῃσιν.
Ὣς ἄρα τήκετο γαῖα σέλαι πυρὸς αἰθομένοιο.
Ῥῖψε δέ μιν θυμῷ ἀκαχὼν ἐς Τάρταρον εὐρύν.
Ἐκ δὲ Τυφωέος ἔστ' ἀνέμων μένος ὑγρὸν ἀέντων,
νόσφι Νότου Βορέωτε καὶ ἀργέστεω Ζεφύροιο· 870
οἵ γε μὲν ἐκ θεόφιν γενεή, θνητοῖς μέγ' ὄνειαρ·
Οἱ δ' ἄλλοι μαψαῦραι ἐπιπνείουσι θάλασσαν·
αἵ δή τοι πίπτουσαι ἐς ἠεροειδέα πόντον,
πῆμα μέγα θνητοῖσι, κακῇ θυίουσιν ἀέλλῃ
ἄλλοτε δ' ἄλλαι ἄεισι διασκιδνᾶσί τε νῆας 875
ναύτας τε φθείρουσι· κακοῦ δ' οὐ γίγνεται ἀλκὴ
ἀνδράσιν, οἵ κείνῃσι συνάντωνται κατὰ πόντον·
αἵ δ' αὖ καὶ κατὰ γαῖαν ἀπείριτον ἀνθεμόεσσαν
ἔργ' ἐρατὰ φθείρουσι χαμαιγενέων ἀνθρώπων
πιμπλεῖσαι κόνιός τε καὶ ἀργαλέου κολοσυρτοῦ. 880
Αὐτὰρ ἐπεί ῥα πόνον μάκαρες θεοὶ ἐξετέλεσσαν,
Τιτήνεσσι δὲ τιμάων κρίναντο βίηφι,
δή ῥα τότ' ὤτρυνον βασιλευέμεν ἠδὲ ἀνάσσειν
Γαίης φραδμοσύνῃσιν Ὀλύμπιον εὐρύοπα Ζῆν
ἀθανάτων· ὃ δὲ τοῖσιν ἑὰς διεδάσσατο τιμάς. 885
Ζεὺς δὲ θεῶν βασιλεὺς πρώτην ἄλοχον θέτο Μῆτιν

jerked in the dim and steep glens of the mountain 860
when he was smitten. Dreadful and fiery breath scorched
a great part of the giant earth and it was melting as a tin melts
when heated by men's art in well-bored crucibles,
or as iron, which is hardest of all things, when is overpowered
by burning fire in mountain glens and melts in the divine earth, 865
from the palms of Hephaestos's hands. In this way the earth
was melting in the blaze of burning fire.
And in vexed anger, Zeus hurled him into wide Tartaros.
From Typhoeus come the damp blowing of the winds,
Boreas, and clear Zephyr, except Notos. 870
They are of the race of gods, and a great aid to mortals.
The others blow idly over the sea and they are the ones
who fall violently on the open, misty sea, rushing in bad tempest
and are a great suffering to humans. At other times, elsewhere,
blowing chaotically they scatter ships and destroy seamen. 875
There is no defense for men against this evil
when they meet on the open sea.
And again, over the boundless and flowering earth,
they destroy the lovely possessions of the earth-born men,
filling them with dust and rubble. 880
But when the blessed gods had accomplished their toil
and settled by force the honors for the Titanes,
they encouraged the far-seeing Olympian Zeus
to reign and rule over the immortals with Gaia's prompting.
So he distributed honors to them. 885
Then Zeus, king of the gods, made Metis his first wife

πλεῖστα τε ἰδυῖαν ἰδὲ θνητῶν ἀνθρώπων.

ἀλλ᾽ ὅτε δὴ ἄρ᾽ ἔμελλε θεὰν γλαυκῶπιν Ἀθήνην

τέξεσθαι, τότ᾽ ἔπειτα δόλῳ φρένας ἐξαπατήσας

αἱμυλίοισι λόγοισιν ἑὴν ἐσκάτθετο νηδὺν   890

Γαίης φραδμοσύνῃσι καὶ Οὐρανοῦ ἀστερόεντος.

τὼς γάρ οἱ φρασάτην, ἵνα μὴ βασιληίδα τιμὴν

ἄλλος ἔχοι Διὸς ἀντὶ θεῶν αἰειγενετάων.

Ἐκ γὰρ τῆς εἵμαρτο περίφρονα τέκνα γενέσθαι·

πρώτην μὲν κούρην γλαυκώπιδα Τριτογένειαν   895

ἶσον ἔχουσαν πατρὶ μένος καὶ ἐπίφρονα βουλήν.

αὐτὰρ ἔπειτ᾽ ἄρα παῖδα θεῶν βασιλῆα καὶ ἀνδρῶν

ἤμελλεν τέξεσθαι, ὑπέρβιον ἦτορ ἔχοντα·

ἀλλ᾽ ἄρα μιν Ζεὺς πρόσθεν ἑὴν ἐσκάτθετο νηδύν,

ὡς δή οἱ φράσσαιτο θεὰ ἀγαθόν τε κακόν τε.   900

Δεύτερον ἠγάγετο λιπαρὴν Θέμιν, ἣ τέκεν Ὥρας,

Εὐνουμίην τε Δίκην τε καὶ Εἰρήνην τεθαλυῖαν,

αἳ ἔργ᾽ ὠρεύουσι καταθνητοῖσι βροτοῖσι,

Μοίρας θ᾽, ᾗ πλείστην τιμὴν πόρε μητίετα Ζεύς,

Κλωθώ τε Λάχεσίν τε καὶ Ἄτροπον, αἵτε διδοῦσι   905

θνητοῖς ἀνθρώποισιν ἔχειν ἀγαθόν τε κακόν τε.

Τρεῖς δέ οἱ Εὐρυνόμη Χάριτας τέκε καλλιπαρῄους,

Ὠκεανοῦ κούρη, πολυήρατον εἶδος ἔχουσα,

Ἀγλαΐην τε καὶ Εὐφροσύνην Θαλίην τ᾽ ἐρατεινήν·

[τῶν καὶ ἀπὸ βλεφάρων ἔρος εἴβετο δερκομενάων   910

λυσιμελής· καλὸν δέ θ᾽ ὑπ᾽ ὀφρύσι δερκιόωνται.]

Αὐτὰρ ὁ Δήμητρος πολυφόρβης ἐς λέχος ἦλθεν,

ἣ τέκε Περσεφόνην λευκώλενον, ἣν Ἀιδωνεὺς

and she knew the most among gods and mortal men.

But when she was about to bring forth the bright-eyed goddess Athena,

Zeus deceived her mind with flattering words

and placed her for safety in his own paunch, 890

as Gaia and starry Ouranos advised him.

In this way they counseled that no other should hold

royal prerogative over the eternal gods, but only Zeus,

for very wise children were allotted to be born of her,

with first the maiden, glaukopis Tritogeneia, 895

equal to her father in strength and thoughtful determination.

But afterwards, she was going to beget

a child with overwhelming heart,

but Zeus placed her before in his own paunch,

so the goddess shows him both good and evil.* 900

Next, he brought with him shining Themis who bore the Horai (hours)

and Eunomia (order), Dike (justice), and blooming Eirene (peace)

who take care of the works of mortal men,

and Moirai (fates) to whom wise Zeus gave the greatest honor,

Klotho, Lakhesis, and Atropos, who give both good and evil to mortal men to have. 905

And Eurenome, the daughter of Okeanos, very lovely in form,

bore him three fair-cheeked Kharites (graces),

Aglaea, Euphrosene, and lovely Thaleia,

from whose eyes as they were glancing,

limb-relaxing love was trickling down 910

and they can see the noble under their brows.

Also, he came to bed with all-nourishing Demeter

and she bore white-armed Persephone, whom Aidoneus (Hades)

ἥρπασε ἧς παρὰ μητρός· ἔδωκε δὲ μητίετα Ζεύς.
Μνημοσύνης δ᾽ ἐξαῦτις ἐράσσατο καλλικόμοιο, 915
ἐξ ἧς οἱ Μοῦσαι χρυσάμπυκες ἐξεγένοντο
ἐννέα, τῆισιν ἅδον θαλίαι καὶ τέρψις ἀοιδῆς.
Λητὼ δ᾽ Ἀπόλλωνα καὶ Ἄρτεμιν ἰοχέαιραν,
ἱμερόεντα γόνον περὶ πάντων Οὐρανιώνων,
γείνατο, αἰγιόχοιο Διὸς φιλότητι μιγεῖσα. 920
Λοισθοτάτην δ᾽ Ἥρην θαλερὴν ποιήσατ᾽ ἄκοιτιν
ἣ δ᾽ Ἥβην καὶ Ἄρηα καὶ Εἰλείθυιαν ἔτικτε
μιχθεῖσ᾽ ἐν φιλότητι θεῶν βασιλῆι καὶ ἀνδρῶν.
Αὐτὸς δ᾽ ἐκ κεφαλῆς γλαυκώπιδα Τριτογένειαν
δεινὴν ἐγρεκύδοιμον ἀγέστρατον ἀτρυτώνην 925
πότνιαν, ἧι κέλαδοί τε ἅδον πόλεμοί τε μάχαι τε,
Ἥρη δ᾽ Ἥφαιστον κλυτὸν οὐ φιλότητι μιγεῖσα
γείνατο, καὶ ζαμένησε καὶ ἤρισε ᾧ παρακοίτῃ,
ἐκ πάντων τέχνηισι κεκασμένον Οὐρανιώνων.
Ἐκ δ᾽ Ἀμφιτρίτης καὶ ἐρικτύπου Ἐννοσιγαίου 930
Τρίτων εὐρυβίης γένετο μέγας, ὅστε θαλάσσης
πυθμέν᾽ ἔχων παρὰ μητρὶ φίλῃ καὶ πατρὶ ἄνακτι
ναίει χρύσεα δῶ, δεινὸς θεός. αὐτὰρ Ἄρηι
ῥινοτόρῳ Κυθέρεια Φόβον καὶ Δεῖμον ἔτικτε
δεινούς, οἵτ᾽ ἀνδρῶν πυκινὰς κλονέουσι φάλαγγας 935
ἐν πολέμῳ κρυόεντι σὺν Ἄρηι πτολιπόρθῳ,
Ἁρμονίην θ᾽, ἣν Κάδμος ὑπέρθυμος θέτ᾽ ἄκοιτιν.
Ζηνὶ δ᾽ ἄρ᾽ Ἀτλαντὶς Μαίη τέκε κύδιμον Ἑρμῆν,
κήρυκ᾽ ἀθανάτων, ἱερὸν λέχος εἰσαναβᾶσα.
Καδμείη δ᾽ ἄρα οἱ Σεμέλη τέκε φαίδιμον υἱὸν 940

snatched away from her mother, but all-wise Zeus gave her to him.

And again, he fell in love with beautiful-haired Mnemosyne, 915

and of her the nine gold-crowned Mousai were born,

who are delighted with festivities and the pleasure of singing.

And Leto, falling in love with aigiokhos Zeus,

bore Apollo and the arrow-shooter, Artemis,

delightsome children of all the sons of Ouranos. 920

Last of all, he made blooming Hera his wife

and she brought forth Hebe, Ares, and Eileithyia

when she joined in love with the king of gods and men.

But he himself brought into being from his own head bright-eyed Tritogeneia

the powerful, the din, the war-rouser, the host-leader, the unwearying, 925

the queen who delights in dins and wars and battles.

Then Hera, without union with Zeus, for she was very angry

and quarrelled with her spouse, bore famous Hephaistos,

who excelled above all the sons of Ouranos in crafts.

And of Amphitrite and the loud-sounding earth-shaker 930

was born Trito the mighty, who possesses the depths of the sea,

living with his dear mother and his lord father

in their golden houses, a fearful god. Also, Kytherea (Aphrodite)

bore to Aris the shield-piercer, Phobos and Deimos, terrible gods

who drive in confusion the compact ranks of men in chilling war 935

with the help of the city-sacker Ares and Harmonia,

whom high-spirited Kadmos made his wife.

And Atlantis Maia, going up to a divine bed,

bore to Zeus glorious Hermes, messenger of the immortals.

And the daughter of Kadmos Semele joined in love with Zeus 940

μιχθεῖσ' ἐν φιλότητι, Διώνυσον πολυγηθέα,

ἀθάνατον θνητή· νῦν δ' ἀμφότεροι θεοί εἰσιν.

Ἀλκμήνη δ' ἄρ' ἔτικτε βίην Ἡρακληείην

μιχθεῖσ' ἐν φιλότητι Διὸς νεφεληγερέταο.

Ἀγλαΐην δ' Ἥφαιστος, ἀγακλυτὸς ἀμφιγυήεις, 945

ὁπλοτάτην Χαρίτων θαλερὴν ποιήσατ' ἄκοιτιν.

Χρυσοκόμης δὲ Διώνυσος ξανθὴν Ἀριάδνην,

κούρην Μίνωος, θαλερὴν ποιήσατ' ἄκοιτιν.

Τὴν δέ οἱ ἀθάνατον καὶ ἀγήρω θῆκε Κρονίων.

Ἥβην δ' Ἀλκμήνης καλλισφύρου ἄλκιμος υἱός, 950

ἲς Ἡρακλῆος, τελέσας στονόεντας ἀέθλους,

παῖδα Διὸς μεγάλοιο καὶ Ἥρης χρυσοπεδίλου,

αἰδοίην θέτ' ἄκοιτιν ἐν Οὐλύμπῳ νιφόεντι,

ὄλβιος, ὃς μέγα ἔργον ἐν ἀθανάτοισιν ἀνύσσας

ναίει ἀπήμαντος καὶ ἀγήραος ἤματα πάντα. 955

Ἡελίῳ δ' ἀκάμαντι τέκεν κλυτὸς Ὠκεανίνη

Περσηὶς Κίρκην τε καὶ Αἰήτην βασιλῆα.

Αἰήτης δ' υἱὸς φαεσιμβρότου Ἡελίοιο

κούρην Ὠκεανοῖο τελήεντος ποταμοῖο

γῆμε θεῶν βουλῇσι, Ἰδυῖαν καλλιπάρηον. 960

ἣ δέ οἱ Μήδειαν εὔσφυρον ἐν φιλότητι

γείναθ' ὑποδμηθεῖσα διὰ χρυσέην Ἀφροδίτην.

Ἡμεῖς μὲν νῦν χαίρετ', Ὀλύμπια δώματ' ἔχοντες,

νῆσοί τ' ἤπειροί τε καὶ ἁλμυρὸς ἔνδοθι πόντος.

Νῦν δὲ θεάων φῦλον ἀείσατε, ἡδυέπειαι 965

Μοῦσαι Ὀλυμπιάδες, κοῦραι Διὸς αἰγιόχοιο,

ὅσσαι δὴ θνητοῖσι παρ' ἀνδράσιν εὐνηθεῖσαι

and bore a shining son, delightful Dionysos. Mortal woman

with an immortal son, and now they are both gods.

And Alkmene bore mighty Herakles

when she joined in love with Zeus the cloud-thunderer.

And Hephaistos, the famous lame one, 945

made the youngest of the Kharites, blooming Aglaea, his wife.

And golden-haired Dionysos made the blond-haired Ariadne,

the daughter of Minos, his flourishing wife,

and the son of Kronos made her immortal and undecaying for him.

And heroic Herakles, the mighty son of neat-ankled Alkmene, 950

when he had finished mournful tasks made Hebe,

the child of great Zeus and gold-sandaled Hera,

his venerable wife in snowy Olympos. Now, there he lives happy,

unharmed, and at all times undecaying

because he did accomplish great work for the immortals. 955

And Perseis, daughter of Okeanos, bore to untiring Helios

Kirke and Aeetes the king.

And Aeetes, the son of Helios who brings light to mortals,

married the beautiful-cheeked Idyia,

daughter of Okeanos, the perfect river, by the will of the gods: 960

and being subject to him in love through golden Aphrodite,

bore him beautiful-ankled Medea.

And now farewell, you who have Olympian homes,

and you islands and continents, and you distasteful sea within.

Now sweet-voiced Mousai of Olympos, 965

daughters of aegiokhos Zeus, sing about the race

of immortal goddesses who laid with mortal men

ἀθάναται γείναντο θεοῖς ἐπιείκελα τέκνα.

Δημήτηρ μὲν Πλοῦτον ἐγείνατο, δῖα θεάων,

Ἰασίων᾽ ἥρωι μιγεῖσ᾽ ἐρατῇ φιλότητι   970

νειῷ ἔνι τριπόλῳ, Κρήτης ἐν πίονι δήμῳ,

ἐσθλόν, ὃς εἶσ᾽ ἐπὶ γῆν τε καὶ εὐρέα νῶτα θαλάσσης

πάντη· τῷ δὲ τυχόντι καὶ οὗ κ᾽ ἐς χεῖρας ἵκηται,

τὸν δ᾽ ἀφνειὸν ἔθηκε, πολὺν δέ οἱ ὤπασεν ὄλβον.

Κάδμῳ δ᾽ Ἁρμονίη, θυγάτηρ χρυσέης Ἀφροδίτης,   975

Ἰνὼ καὶ Σεμέλην καὶ Ἀγαυὴν καλλιπάρηον

Αὐτονόην θ᾽, ἣν γῆμεν Ἀρισταῖος βαθυχαίτης,

γείνατο καὶ Πολύδωρον ἐυστεφάνῳ ἐνὶ Θήβῃ.

[Κούρη δ᾽ Ὠκεανοῦ, Χρυσάορι καρτεροθύμῳ

μιχθεῖσ᾽ ἐν φιλότητι πολυχρύσου Ἀφροδίτης,   980

Καλλιρόη τέκε παῖδα βροτῶν κάρτιστον ἁπάντων,

Γηρυονέα, τὸν κτεῖνε βίη Ἡρακληείη

βοῶν ἕνεκ᾽ εἰλιπόδων ἀμφιρρύτῳ εἰν Ἐρυθείῃ.]

Τιθωνῷ δ᾽ Ἠὼς τέκε Μέμνονα χαλκοκορυστήν,

Αἰθιόπων βασιλῆα, καὶ Ἠμαθίωνα ἄνακτα.   985

Αὐτὰρ ὑπαὶ Κεφάλῳ φιτύσατο φαίδιμον υἱόν,

ἴφθιμον Φαέθοντα, θεοῖς ἐπιείκελον ἄνδρα.

Τόν ῥα νέον τέρεν ἄνθος ἔχοντ᾽ ἐρικυδέος ἥβης

παῖδ᾽ ἀταλὰ φρονέοντα φιλομμειδὴς Ἀφροδίτη

ὦρτ᾽ ἀναρεψαμένη, καί μιν ζαθέοις ἐνὶ νηοῖς   990

νηοπόλον νύχιον ποιήσατο, δαίμονα δῖον.

Κούρην δ᾽ Αἰήταο διοτρεφέος βασιλῆος

Αἰσονίδης βουλῇσι θεῶν αἰειγενετάων

ἦγε παρ᾽ Αἰήτεω, τελέσας στονόεντας ἀέθλους,

τοὺς πολλοὺς ἐπέτελλε μέγας βασιλεὺς ὑπερήνωρ,   995

and brought forth children who are like gods.
Demeter, the noblest of goddesses,
being united in sweet love with the hero Iason 970
in a thrice-ploughed field, in the rich land of Krete,
bore Ploutos, a wealthy god who goes everywhere on land
and the wide surface of the sea, and whoever by chance
holds him in his hands, Ploutos makes him rich,
giving great wealth upon him. 975
And Harmonia, the daughter of golden Aphrodite,
bore to Kadmus, Ino, and Semele, and beautiful-cheeked Agaue
and Autonoe whom long-haired Aristaios wedded,
and also Polydoros in Thebe, crowned with walls and towers.
And the daughter of Okeanos, Kallirhoe, joined in love 980
with stout-hearted Khrysaor because of the rich-in-gold Aphrodite,
and bore a child who was the strongest of all men, Gereones,
whom strong Herakles did kill in sea-girt Erythea for his reeling oxen.
And Eos bore to Tithonos brass-armed Memnon,
king of the Ethiopians, and the lord Emathion. 985
And to Kephalos she bore a shining son, strong Phaethon,
a man like the gods, whom when he was youthful
in the smooth flower of glorious youth and tender-minded,
laughter-loving Aphrodite rushed and snatched him up
and made him a temple-keeper, 990
inmost of her holy shrine by night, a divine spirit.
By the will of the everlasting gods, the son of Aison
led away the daughter of king Aeetes, himself cherished by Zeus,
when he had completed many mournful labors
which the great king Pelias the overbearing, 995

ὑβριστὴς Πελίης καὶ ἀτάσθαλος, ὀβριμοεργός.

τοὺς τελέσας Ἰαωλκὸν ἀφίκετο, πολλὰ μογήσας,

ὠκείης ἐπὶ νηὸς ἄγων ἑλικώπιδα κούρην

Αἰσονίδης, καί μιν θαλερὴν ποιήσατ' ἄκοιτιν.

Καί ῥ' ἥ γε δμηθεῖσ' ὑπ' Ἰήσονι, ποιμένι λαῶν, 1000

Μήδειον τέκε παῖδα, τὸν οὔρεσιν ἔτρεφε Χείρων

Φιλυρίδης· μεγάλου δὲ Διὸς νόος ἐξετελεῖτο.

Αὐτὰρ Νηρῆος κοῦραι, ἁλίοιο γέροντος,

ἦ τοι μὲν Φῶκον Ψαμάθη τέκε δῖα θεάων

Αἰακοῦ ἐν φιλότητι διὰ χρυσέην Ἀφροδίτην, 1005

Πηλέι δὲ δμηθεῖσα θεὰ Θέτις ἀργυρόπεζα

γείνατ' Ἀχιλλῆα ῥηξήνορα θυμολέοντα.

Αἰνείαν δ' ἄρ' ἔτικτεν ἐυστέφανος Κυθέρεια

Ἀγχίσῃ ἥρωι μιγεῖσ' ἐρατῇ φιλότητι

Ἴδης ἐν κορυφῇσι πολυπτύχου ὑληέσσης. 1010

Κίρκη δ', Ἠελίου θυγάτηρ Ὑπεριονίδαο,

γείνατ' Ὀδυσσῆος ταλασίφρονος ἐν φιλότητι

Ἄγριον ἠδὲ Λατῖνον ἀμύμονά τε κρατερόν τε·

[Τηλέγονον δ' ἄρ' ἔτικτε διὰ χρυσέην Ἀφροδίτην.]

οἳ δή τοι μάλα τῆλε μυχῷ νήσων ἱεράων 1015

πᾶσιν Τυρσηνοῖσιν ἀγακλειτοῖσιν ἄνασσον.

Ναυσίθοον δ' Ὀδυσῆι Καλυψὼ δῖα θεάων

γείνατο Ναυσίνοόν τε μιγεῖσ' ἐρατῇ φιλότητι.

Αὗται μὲν θνητοῖσι παρ' ἀνδράσιν εὐνηθεῖσαι

ἀθάναται γείναντο θεοῖς ἐπιείκελα τέκνα. 1020

Νῦν δὲ γυναικῶν φῦλον ἀείσατε, ἡδυέπειαι

Μοῦσαι Ὀλυμπιάδες, κοῦραι Διὸς αἰγιόχοιο. 1022

the wanton, the arrogant and violent, commanded.

When the son of Aison had accomplished these tasks, he came to Iolkos

after long toil with his swift ship, bringing the quick-glancing girl with him

and making her his blooming wife.

And her, been subdued to the shepherd of people, Iason, 1000

bore a child, Medeos, whom Kheiron, the son of Philyros,

brought up in the mountains, and the intentions of great Zeus were fulfilled.

But the daughter of Nereus, the old man of the sea,

Psamanthe, the divine goddess, was loved by Aiakos

through golden Aphrodite and bore Phokos, 1005

and the silver-footed goddess Thetis, having been conquered by Peleus,

brought forth lion-hearted Akhilleus, the armed rank-breaker.

And beautiful-crowned Kytherea joined in sweet love

with hero Ankhises and bore Aenias

on the peaks of windy and with many foldings Ida. 1010

And Kirke, the daughter of Helios who is the Hyperion's son,

fell in love with stout-hearted Odysseus and bore

Agrios and the noble and strong Latinos.

Also, she brought forth Telegonos by the will of golden Aphrodite.

They ruled over the famous Tyrenians, 1015

very far in the inmost of the holy islands.

The divine goddess Kalypso was joined to Odysseus in sweet love

and bore him Nausithoos and Nausinoos.

These are the goddesses who did lay with mortal men

and brought forth children like gods. 1020

But now, sweet-voiced Olympian Mousai,*

daughters of aegiokhos Zeus, sing for the race of women. 1022

Notes

2. Because Hesiod is introduced as having been visited by the Mousai at Mount Helikon, Helikon becomes synonymous with poetic inspiration in the Western literary tradition forever after.

3. I am not literally translating it as "soft or tender feet" but as a metaphor, which means "gentle feet" to indicate dancing softly. On the eighth verse the mode of the dance changes to rapid and vigorous, with all their strength on their feet.

13. The adjective *glaukopis* literally means "owl-faced" or "owl-eyed"; over time, through association with Athena, it came to mean "blue-eyed" or "grey-eyed" or "bright-eyed" and it is a very familiar description of Athena. How it got from "owl" to "blue-grey-bright" is an interesting question. The epithet remains as is and it is upon the reader's choice, the same as with one of the most common epithets of Zeus, *aegiokhos*, which literally means "shield-bearing" or "shield-holder." The shield is a defensive weapon that offers protection. Since Zeus was not the only one bearing a shield, to be distinguished with this name and being the father of gods and man, he should be able to provide protection to his children under the aegis. As for today, the term "under the aegis of" means "under the protection of." To my opinion then, *aegiokhos* is a metaphor meaning "protector."

22, 31. The Mousai teach and inspire Hesiod, and his poetic talent becomes a spiritual project for them, giving him the authority to compose and publish the song.

28. How true are myths? Let us leave this up to the reader's judgment once s/he sees the definitions, the similarities, and the differences between myth and logos (reason). In my opinion, myth has a metaphorical meaning, but logos is specific and definite.

Hesiod Theogony 800–700 BC

Myth

- Anything delivered by word or mouth
- Word
- Speech
- Speech in the public assembly
- Talk
- Conversation
- Counsel
- Advice
- Command
- Order
- Promise
- A saying
- The talk of men
- Rumor
- Tale
- Story
- Narrative
- Legend
- Historic table
- Fable

Logos

- The word that by which the inward thought is expressed
- Ratio (Latin)
- Word
- Talk
- Saying
- Conversation
- Statement
- Maxim
- Promise
- Command
- Speech
- Discourse
- Mention
- Reason
- Report
- Repute
- Language
- Tale
- Story
- Fictitious story
- Fable
- Narrative
- Oration
- Opinion
- Expectation
- Account
- Consideration
- Esteem
- Regard
- Proportion
- Analogy
- Report
- Repute
- Language
- Tale
- Story
- Fictitious story
- Fable
- Narrative
- Oration
- Opinion
- Expectation
- Account
- Consideration
- Esteem
- Regard
- Proportion
- Analogy

78   Metaphrasis: Dimitrios Kiriakopoulos

35. But why all of this around an oak and a stone?
   This metaphoric verse clearly and simply means "away from people" or "away in the wilderness." The phrase is also used in the modern Greek language meaning "deserted area."

—*Dimitris Kiriakopoulos*

35. But what is this of oak or rock to me?
   This puzzling line must be a proverb of some kind. The meaning may be "Why do I speak further of incredible things?" (i.e., the epiphany of the Muses), but this cannot be demonstrated. At any rate, the verse is an indication that one topic is ending and another is about to begin.

—*R. Caldwell*

35. But why all this about oak or stone?
   A proverbial saying meaning "Why enlarge on irrelevant topics?"

—*Hugh G. Evelyn-White*

35. But what is my business round tree or rock?

—*M. L. West*

35. No more delays; begin:

—*Dorothea Wender*

38. The Mousai have knowledge of the present and past and are also able to see the future.

76. *«Διός εκγεγαυίαι.» According to Liddell and Scott's *Lexicon*, it means: "To be born of Zeus," not "begotten of Zeus." That raises questions, such as if the mother, Mnemosyne, bore the daughters, or if she just conceived them and on continuation, Zeus bore them somehow, just as it happened with Athena and Dionysos; considering the educational role they served for the people, he wanted to make sure they became very wise and responsible. The phrase corresponds to Homer's account of the *Iliad* 2.597 FF and *Odyssey* 8.457 FF and this is most likely to be the daughters born from Zeus.

77. Mousai are the keepers and guards of the ancient archives (museums) of the oral and written logos (speech).

- Kleio: Muse of history and poetry. She is often represented with a parchment scroll or a set of tablets, and is also known as "the proclaimer."
- Euterpe: Muse of music and lyric poetry. She is depicted holding a flute, and she invented the double flute. Her name derived from the words *eu-* and *terpo*, "giver of delight."
- Melpomene: Theatre and chorus muse. She is portrayed holding a tragic mask or sword and sometimes wearing a wreath of ivy. Her name derived from the verb *melpo*, meaning "to celebrate with dance and song."
- Terpsikhore: Muse of choral song and dancing. She is represented with plectrum and lyre. Her name derived from *terpsis* and *chorus*, "delighting in dance."
- Polymnia: Muse of religious hymns. Her name means "many hymns." She is depicted usually looking up to the sky holding a lyre and being wrapped in a robe. Because of her great praises she brings distinction to writers whose works achieved for them immortal fame.
- Kalliopi: Muse of epic poetry. She is always seen with a writing tablet in her hand. Sometimes she is carrying a roll of paper or a book, and wearing a gold crown.

- Thalia: Muse of comedy and idyllic poetry. She is portrayed as a young woman crowned with ivy, holding a comic mask.
- Erato: Muse of erotic poetry. Her name means "beloved." She is often shown with myrtle wreath and roses, holding a lyre or a kithara.
- Ourania: Muse of astronomy. Her name means "of the heavens." She is usually depicted with the globe in her left hand. She is able to foretell the future by the arrangement of the stars and she is associated with universal love and the holy spirit. She is dressed in a cloak embroidered with stars and she keeps her eyes focused on the sky. Those who study philosophy and astronomy are dearest to her.

116. The Mousai start the narration with the cosmogonic event that doesn't differ from the so-called "Big Bang." At first, Khaos was created: the first state of the universe and the infinite space fulfilled with fused elements, fit for further creations.

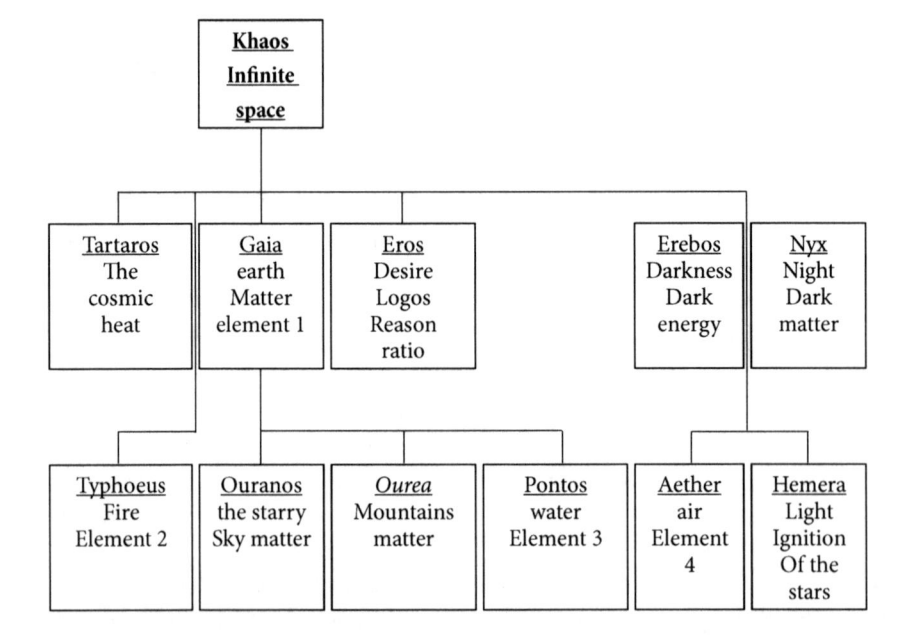

```
                    ┌─────────────┐
                    │   Khaos     │
                    │  Infinite   │
                    │   space     │
                    └──────┬──────┘
   ┌─────────┬─────────────┼─────────────┬──────────┬─────────┐
┌──┴───┐ ┌───┴──┐  ┌───────┴──┐    ┌─────┴───┐  ┌───┴───┐
│Tartaros│ │ Gaia │  │   Eros   │    │ Erebos  │  │  Nyx  │
│  The   │ │earth │  │  Desire  │    │Darkness │  │ Night │
│ cosmic │ │Matter│  │  Logos   │    │  Dark   │  │ Dark  │
│  heat  │ │elem 1│  │  Reason  │    │ energy  │  │matter │
│        │ │      │  │   ratio  │    │         │  │       │
└────────┘ └──┬───┘  └──────────┘    └────┬────┘  └───────┘
    ┌─────────┼──────────┬──────────┐      ┌──┴──────┐
┌───┴────┐┌───┴───┐┌─────┴───┐┌─────┴──┐┌──┴────┐┌───┴────┐
│Typhoeus││Ouranos││  Ourea  ││ Pontos ││Aether ││Hemera  │
│  Fire  ││ starry││Mountains││ water  ││  air  ││ Light  │
│Element2││Sky mat││ matter  ││Element3││Elem 4 ││Ignition│
│        ││       ││         ││        ││       ││Of the  │
│        ││       ││         ││        ││       ││ stars  │
└────────┘└───────┘└─────────┘└────────┘└───────┘└────────┘
```

120. Eros is placed in the first state of the creation. Being Aphrodite's child, obviously he was born much later. If someone observes the word carefully, he can think it could be the "logos: the divine rational principle," the fundamental reason of everything. Logos is a noun created from the verb in present tense λέγω (*lego*). *Eros* is the noun of the same verb, which is in the future tense ερώ(*ero*). Another fact that shows they are different is that Aphrodite's child is spelled Ερως with the Omega, yet the first Ερος is spelled with an Omicron.

148. "Not renowned." This phrase has been wrongly translated by many translators as "who can't be named," or "beyond telling," or "it is worthless mentioning their name," et cetera. This is the wrong approach. The names are mentioned. They are: Kottos, Briareos, and Gyes, and they are also called magnificent and powerful children. The phrase literally means "not renowned," "not that famous," "unknown," because they showed their power only in the war against the Titanes.

162. Adamantite is the hardest type of iron called cast iron, and sometimes "diamond" for its hardness. Using this metal, Hesiod wants to show the gravity of the attempt and with the tool that Kronos uses, he is able to overcome any resistance. "Pruning-hook" is mostly translated as "jagged sickle." A sickle won't do much for a job like that, for a sickle is good to cut grass and wheat. What is needed to cut "branches" is a curved, sharp tool, which is the pruning-hook and being jagged won't help much. This is a comparison with the shark's teeth for its sharpness. Then we literally have, "the cast iron, sharp pruning-hook."

211. Kronos overtakes power with a coup, by the help of his mother. From the time of this "political crime," the forces of evil prevail and we see all the evil and painful deities lining up as soon as Kronos took over.

216. Hesiod repeatedly makes a clear statement of the land that is beyond the famous ocean with the three thousand islands, which are very difficult to be named one by one, but they are known to the people who dwell all around. That is how it is reported by the poet, who clearly avoids to call by its name this very important region, although he has

a name for everything. My explanation is because of his excessive fear. We all avoid calling awful things by name to indicate our dislike.

Plato on "Timaeus 25a" calls it a continent.

From this island (Atlantis), travelers in those days could reach the other islands and from them the opposite continent, which surrounds what can truly be called the ocean.

We see the clear view they had of the world, passing the strait of Gibraltar.

498. Accepting Ouranos's accusations that the Titan regime will be evil and rotten, then the setting of the stone in Pytho (*pytho* literally means to become rotten, to decay) at the navel of the earth is the mark of the beginning of a new era by Zeus.

529. Athena was the pride of Zeus amongst the immortals, and Herakles amongst the mortals. He wasn't named Dio-kles or Zeu-kles but Hera-kles (Hera's glory), probably to provoke and challenge his wife, Hera, for begetting his most famous son with another woman. And this is why Hera hated Herakles the most of anyone else.

Herakles lived his life as the greatest hero of all time and when he was about to die, Zeus snatched and placed him among the immortal gods on Olympos.

585. Hesiod's views are not so flattering for women, naming them "beautiful evil," although the poet recognizes that the unmarried life is not the right solution. He insists that to find the perfect wife is a very difficult thing and very rarely is the attempt successful.

625. Earth has the main role and she is the top adviser of the big changes that are supposed to take place. We saw that on the degradation of Ouranos, who had been removed of power by Kronos, according to her plan.

Now is the time for Kronos to be replaced for being corrupted and arrogant according to her plan again, for Mother Earth doesn't agree with ruinous acts and she always reacts accordingly to any mischievousness. As for today, we are responsible for our Mother Earth, and we should take care of our "home," and our actions. We don't know the magnitude of the avenge to be taken from Earth when the corruption and haughtiness reaches the deadline. What power will be used to set the milestone in *Pytho* to signal the end of the old and the beginning of the new era?

674. Hesiod, in a shocking report, like a war correspondent describes the last and final battle between the Olympian gods and the Titans. The good prevails over the bad and Titans (the ones who committed big and arrogant sins) get locked in Tartaros for a long period of time.

723. "Anvil Falling" is the famous "as above so below" of "The Emerald Tablets" by Hermes Trismegistos. "That which is above is the same as that which is below: Macrocosmos is the same as microcosmos, the universe is the same as God, God is the same as man, man is the same as the cell, the cell is the same as the atom, the atom is the same as... and so on." Heracleitos put it as "The way up and the way down is one and the same"; also, "One is all and all is one."

The lines 723, 724, and 725, are all a periphrastic pleonasm of the two previous lines. This is common in epic poetry. We find repetitions throughout the text whenever the poet wants to give emphasis to a matter. For example, the beginning of *Theogony* is redundant by explaining on the second line why the *Mousai* are named *Helikoniadai*.

In this periphrastic repeat, at first, Hesiod describes the space and then the time it takes to go from Earth to Tartaros. Why is he using the infrequent phrase "brazen anvil," a phrase that it is not found in almost the entire ancient Greek literature, and what is the meaning of the metaphor?

With another approach, which may be controversial, the word *akmon*, along with the translation as "anvil," is also a kind of an eagle,

Zeus's symbol of sovereignty. If we translate it as "eagle," then we have a completely different meaning: "For a brazen eagle coming down from sky…"

900. I translate it as "he placed her for safety in his own paunch" ignoring the explanation that one of her children will overthrow Zeus from power. That brings us back to Kronos's tactics.

Athena when born from Zeus was "equal to her father in strength and thoughtful determination" and she never showed any desire to seize power from her father although she was the most powerful among the gods (even the god of war, Ares, was defeated by Athena in a competition). Zeus never tried to limit her power at a certain level, but she was his pride and she was free to express her wisdom and strength where and when she wanted.

So Metis, being the goddess of wisdom and prudence, was "deposited for safety in him to show both good and bad." In other words, his first wife (for he had too many) was his top adviser and the two became one. "Metieta Zeus" is one of his many surnames as leader and creator of the universal civilization.

1021. The story starts with "Helikoniadai" and ends with "Olympian Mousai." The apotheosis gives them a seat among the immortal gods of Mount Olympos.

Related Extracts

"All intellectual teaching and education comes from pre-existed knowledge."
—Aristotle, *The Organon*

Approaching philosophically the universal creation, I considered it necessary to include some extracts of Plato's *Timaeus* and Plutarch's *On Isis and Osiris*, which may trigger the intellectual and noetic abilities of the reader for further thoughts and observations of cosmogonic events.

The Logos, "Reason"

(28a) To my opinion, then, must first be one definition. What is that which eternally is a being and has no becoming, and what is that which is eternally becoming and never is a being? The first one is embraced by intelligence and reason for being always immutable. The second is conceived by opinion and the help of the irrational sense, is always in a process of becoming and perishing, and is indeed never a being. And again, everything that becomes, must of necessity be created by some reason, for without a reason nothing can be created. Whenever, then, the creator looks at the unchangeable and gives the form and power using the unchangeable pattern, the result by necessity will be perfect, but when he looks to the created only and he uses a created pattern, the result will not be perfect.

For the entire sky or cosmos, whether called by this or any other more appropriate name, let's think first which has to be at the beginning of any enquiry, if it always existed without having a beginning, or was created starting from any beginning.

Is a being created, for he is visible and tangible and having a body and therefore sensible and all sentient beings are apprehended by opinion and sense and they come into being created and becoming. Now, we affirm, that which is created is created of necessity by reason.

It is troublesome for the maker and father of this entire universe to be found and if he is found, impossible to tell of him to all men.

The Four Elements

(31b4) Anything that is created must have a body and be visible and tangible, but without fire nothing is visible or tangible if it is not solid, and not solid without earth. For this reason, God started creating the body of the universe with fire and earth. It is not possible only with the two to make it stand well without a third, for a bond is needed to bring them together, and the best bond is the one that becomes successfully one with the bonded bodies. If the body of the universe was supposed to be levelled without depth or height, one intermediate would be enough to bond the parts with itself, but now it has a solid form and the solids are always bonded with two intermediates (never with one). Therefore, God placed water and air between fire and earth and made them analogous to each other. As possible as it could be as the fire is to the air, this much air to the water, and as the air to the water, this much water to the earth. He bound them together and made the visible and tangible sky. Hence, for this reason and these four elements, the body of the world was created to be a unity through analogy and from these, the body acquired friendship to be the same with itself and indissoluble by any, except him who bound it together.

Birth of the Gods

It is beyond our powers to know and tell about the birth of the other divinities. Let's rely on those who have told the story before, who claimed to be children of the Gods and presumably knew about their own ancestors. It is impossible to distrust the children of the Gods, even if they give no likely or necessary proof of what they say. Conforming to the rule, let's believe their account of their own family history. So let's follow them in our account of the birth of these Gods. From Earth and Sky were born two children, Oceanos and Tethys, and from them, Phorkys, Cronos, Rhea, and their companion, and from Cronos and Rhea were born Zeus, Hera, and all who are known as their siblings. They in turn had further descendants.

Therefore, when all the Gods were born, both those who openly wander on the sky and those who only appear to us when they wish, the father of this universe addressed them as follows: "Gods of the

Gods, works whose creator and father I am, what was created by me cannot be dissolved without my wish. Anything bonded together can of course be dissolved, but he is evil whoever wishes to dissolve anything that holds well and well fits together. Therefore, since you have been created, you are not entirely immortal and indissoluble, but you will never be dissolved, nor have the fate of death, for this is my will that is the greatest and supreme bond than those with which you were bound at your birth."

The Triangle Theory

In this section, Plato attempts and succeeds to enter the fields of science and cosmology through philosophy and trigonometry.

(53c4) In the first place, it is clear to everyone that fire, earth, water, and air are bodies and all bodies have depth and, by necessity, the depth is wrapped around by surface and all plane surfaces are composed of triangles.

All triangles derive from two triangles that have one right and two acute angles. One of them has equal sides along each side of the right angle which create equal angles. The other has unequal sides which create unequal angles. This we assume as the principle of fire and the other bodies, proceeding in accordance to the account of likelihood and necessity. The principles that are even higher than these are known to God and whom God loves.

We must say now which would be the four most beautiful bodies, while unlike one another, are capable of transformation into each other on resolution. If we can find this answer, then we know the truth about the creation of earth and fire and the mean terms between them, for we will never agree with anyone that there are visible bodies more beautiful than these, each in its type. So we have to do our best to fit together four types of bodies outstanding for their beauty and maintain that we have grasped their nature sufficiently.

Of the two basic triangles, the isosceles has only one kind, the scalene an infinite number. Let's choose the most beautiful of this infinite number in order to have a good start. If someone can tell us how to choose a more beautiful triangle for the construction of the four bodies, he will prevail not as an enemy, but as a friend.

Overpassing the rest, we postulate one of the many triangles as the most beautiful, that of which a pair compose an equilateral triangle. It would be a long speech to give the reason and if anyone tests and discovers it is so, we will welcome his victory.

So, we choose the two triangles from which fire and the other bodies have been constructed: one isosceles and the other whose square of the greater side is three times the square of the smaller side. We must now clarify something we said unclearly before. It appeared as all four bodies could pass into each other into the process of becoming, but this appearance is misleading because of the four bodies that are produced by our chosen types of triangle, three are composed of the scalene, but the fourth alone from the isosceles. It is not possible, then, to pass into each other on resolution forming a few great and many smaller bodies and vice versa. This can only happen with three of them, for these are all composed of one triangle. When large bodies are broken up, a number of small bodies are formed of the same constituents, taking on their appropriate forms. And when small bodies are broken up into triangles, a single new, larger figure may be formed as they are unified into a solid. So much for their transformation into each other.

(55d8) We must proceed to distribute the figures that have just come into being in our account among fire, earth, water, and air. Let us give the earth the cubic form, for it is the hardest to move of the four and the most malleable of bodies and of necessity, these characteristics belong to the form with the most stable bases. And of the triangles we have posited as principles, the isosceles naturally has a more stable base than the scalene and the equilateral square composed of them, in whole and in part, of necessity is a firmer base than the equilateral triangle. So, by assigning to the earth the cubic form, we preserve the likely account, while we assign the least mobile of the other forms to water, the most mobile to fire, and the intermediate to air. And again, we give the smallest form to fire, the largest to water, the intermediate to air, the sharpest to fire, the next sharpest to air, and the least sharp to water.

Therefore, it is necessary given its nature that the form which has the fewest faces is the most mobile, as well as the sharpest and most penetrating to any direction and the lightest for being composed of the smallest number of identical parts. Our second form will be second to

all these respects, our third will be third. In accordance with the right account and the likely, the solid form we constructed as a pyramid let be the element and seed of fire, and let us say that the second of the forms we constructed is the basic unit of air, and the third of water. We must, of course, think of the individual instances of all four bodies as being far too small to be visible (atoms) and only becoming visible when massed together in large numbers. We must assume that when the bodies had been totally completed, God fitted together their numbers, movements, and their other powers according to whatever way the nature of necessity had been persuaded willingly to yield.

On Isis and Osiris
Plutarch

351C All good things, my dear Clea, sensible men must ask from the Gods, and especially do we pray that from those mighty Gods we may, in our quest, gain knowledge of themselves, so far as such a thing is attainable by men. For we believe that there is nothing more important for man to receive, or more ennobling for God of his grace to grant than the truth. God gives to men the other things for which they express a desire, but of sense and intelligence he grants them only a share, inasmuch as these are his special possessions and his sphere of activity. For the deity is not blessed of his possession of gold and silver, nor strong because of thunder and lightning, but through knowledge and intelligence. Of all the things that Homer said about the Gods, he has expressed most beautifully this thought:
Both, indeed, descend from a common father
but Zeus was the earlier born and his knowledge is greater.

There, he declared that the hegemony of Zeus is more divine, since he is elder in knowledge and in wisdom. I think also that a source of happiness in the eternal life, which is the lot of God, is that events which have happened in the past do not escape his prescience. But if his knowledge and meditation on the nature of existence should be taken away, then his immortality is not life, but duration.

352C It is a fact, Clea, that having a beard and wearing a threadbare cloak does not make philosophers, nor does dressing in linen and shaving the hair make votaries of Isis. But the true votary of Isis is he who, when he has legitimately received what is set forth in the ceremonies connected with these Gods, uses reason in investigating and in studying the truth contained therein.

It is true that most people are unaware of this very ordinary and minor matter: the reason why the priests remove their hair and wear linen garments. Some persons do not care at all to have any knowledge about such things, while others say that the priests, because they revere the sheep, abstain from using its wool as well as its flesh, and that they

shave their heads as a sign of mourning, and that they wear their linen garments because of the color which the flax displays when in bloom, and which is like to the heavenly azure which enfolds the universe. But for all this there is only one true reason, which is to be found in the words of Plato: "For the Impure to touch the Pure is contrary to divine ordinance."

360D5 Better, therefore, is the judgment of those who hold that the stories about Typhon, Osiris, and Isis are records of experiences of neither Gods, nor men, but of demigods, whom Plato and Pythagoras and Xenocrates and Chrysippus, following the lead of early writers on sacred subjects, allege to have been stronger than men and, in their might, greatly surpassing our nature, yet not possessing the divine quality unmixed and uncontaminated, but with a share also in the nature of the soul and in the perceptive faculties of the body, and with a susceptibility to pleasure and pain and to whatsoever other experience is incident to these mutations, and is the source of much disquiet in some and of less in others. For in demigods, as in men, there are different forms of virtue and vice. The exploits of the Giants and Titans celebrated among the Greeks, the lawless deeds of Cronos, the stubborn resistance of Python against Apollo, the flights of Dionysus, and the wanderings of Demeter do not fall at all short of the exploits of Osiris and Typhon and other exploits which anyone may hear freely repeated in traditional story. So, too, all the things which are kept always away from the ears and eyes of the multitude by being concealed behind mystic rites and ceremonies have a similar explanation.

369B Wherefore this very ancient opinion comes down from writers on religion and from lawgivers to poets and philosophers, it can be traced to no source, but it carried a strong and almost indelible conviction, and is in circulation in many places among barbarians and Greeks alike, not only in story and tradition, but also in rites and sacrifices, to the effect that the Universe is not of itself suspended aloft without sense or reason or guidance, nor is there one reason which rules and guides it by rudders, as it were, or by controlling reins, but inasmuch as nature brings in this life of ours, many experiences in which both evil and good are commingled, or better to put it very simply, nature brings nothing which is not combined with something else, we may assert that it is not one keeper of two great vases who, after

the manner of a barmaid, deals out to us our failures and successes in mixture, but it has come about, as the result of two opposed principles and two antagonistic forces, one of which guides us along a straight course to the right, while the other turns us aside and backward, that our life is complex, and so is the universe; if this is not true of the whole of it, yet it is true that this terrestrial universe, including its moon as well, is irregular and variable and subject to all manner of changes. For if it is the law of nature that nothing comes into being without a cause, and if the good cannot provide a cause for evil, then it follows that nature must have in herself the source and origin of evil, just as she contains the source and origin of good.

370E The adherents of Pythagoras include a variety of terms under these categories: under the good they set Unity, the Determinate, the Permanent, the Straight, the Odd, the Square, the Equal, the Right-handed, the Bright; under the bad they set Duality, the Indeterminate, the Moving, the Curved, the Even, the Oblong, the Unequal, the Left-handed, and the Dark, on the supposition that these are the underlying principles of creation. For these, however, Anaxagoras postulates Mind and Infinitude, Aristotle, Form and Privation, and Plato, in many passages, as though obscuring and veiling his opinion, names the one of the opposite principles, "Identity," and the other, "Difference," but in his *Laws*, when he had grown considerably older, he asserts, not in circumlocution or symbolically, but in specific words that the movement of the Universe is actuated not by one soul, but perhaps by several, and certainly by not less than two, and of these the one is beneficent and the other is opposed to it and the artificer of things opposed. Between these, he leaves a certain third nature; not inanimate, nor irrational, nor without the power to move of itself as some think, but with dependence on both those others, and desiring the better always and yearning after it and pursuing it.

About the Author

Dimitrios Kiriakopoulos was born in 1957 and reared in Larisa, Greece where he graduated from high school. A businessman in the food industry, he later relocated to Canada and currently lives in Toronto with his wife and two children.

From a young age he has extensively studied ancient Greek literature and philosophy. The translation of Hesiod's *Theogony* is his first work.